THE STORY OF
CIVILIZATION

VOLUME I
THE ANCIENT WORLD

Activity Book

Copyright © 2016 TAN Books, PO Box 410487, Charlotte, NC 28241.

Cataloging-in-Publication data on file with the Library of Congress.

Illustrations by Chris Pelicano, Caroline Kiser

ISBN: 978-1-5051-0571-1

Printed and bound in the United States of America

THE STORY OF
CIVILIZATION

VOLUME I
THE ANCIENT WORLD

Activity Book

TAN

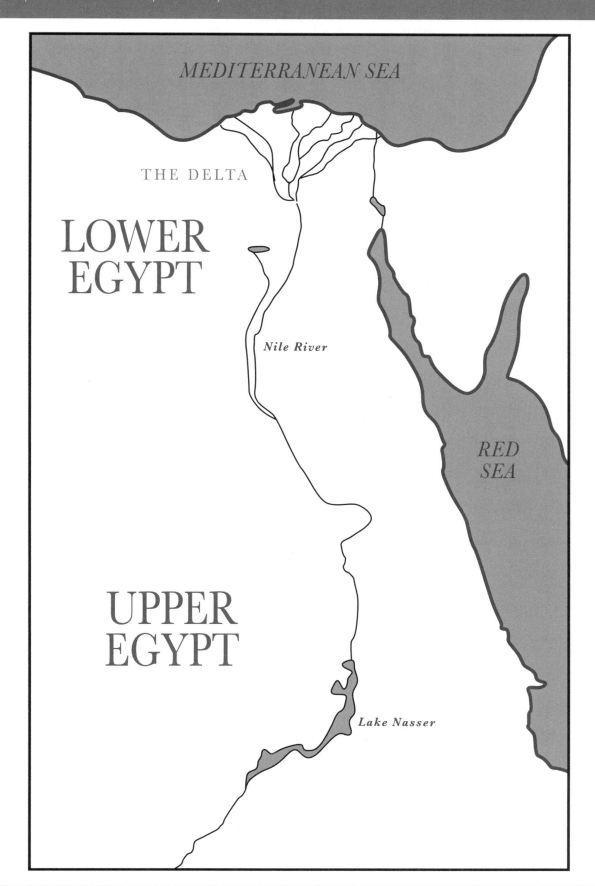

MEDITERRANEAN SEA

THE DELTA

LOWER
EGYPT

Nile River

RED
SEA

UPPER
EGYPT

Lake Nasser

NOTE:
NOT TO SCALE

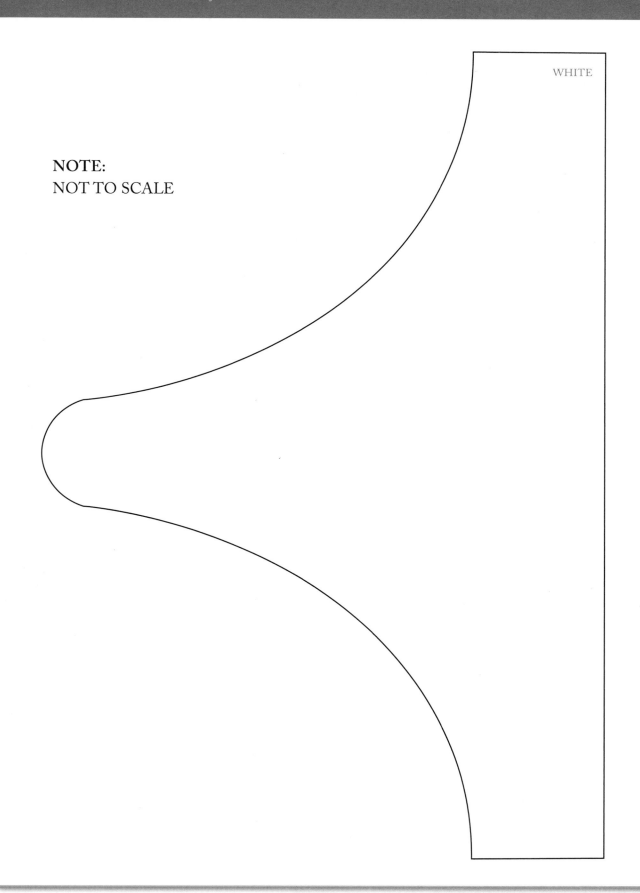

WHITE

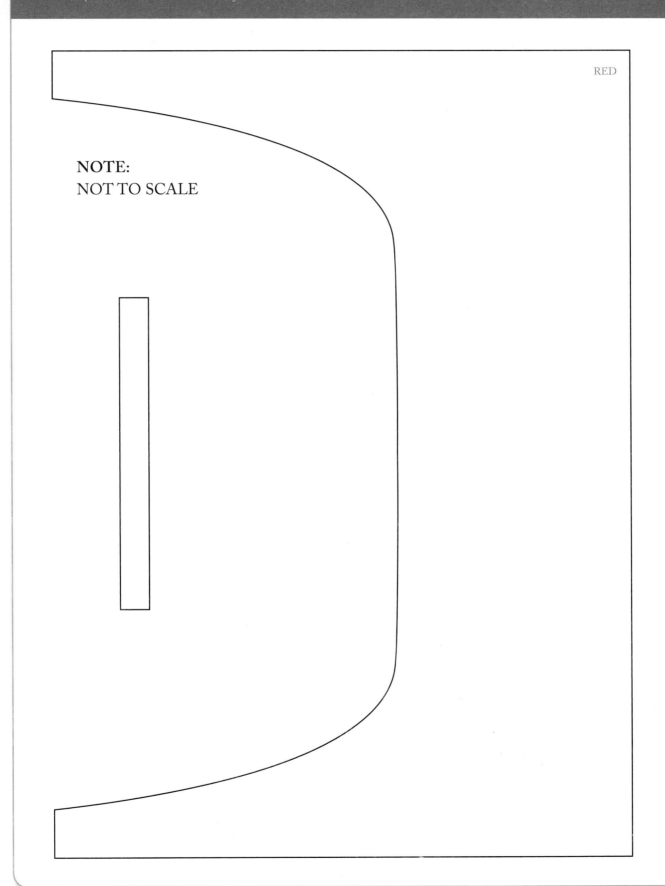

RED

NOTE:
NOT TO SCALE

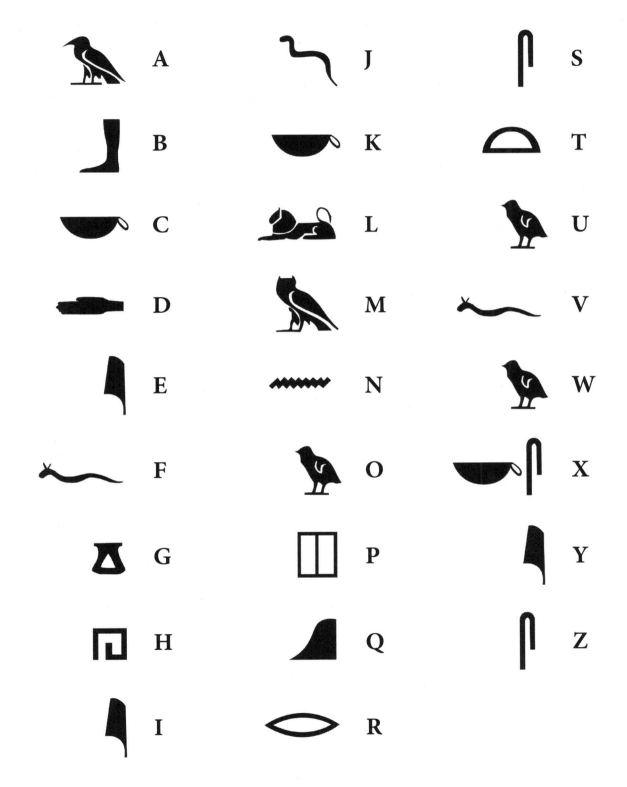

A

B

C

D

E

F

G

H

I

J

K

L

M

N

O

P

Q

R

S

T

U

V

W

X

Y

Z

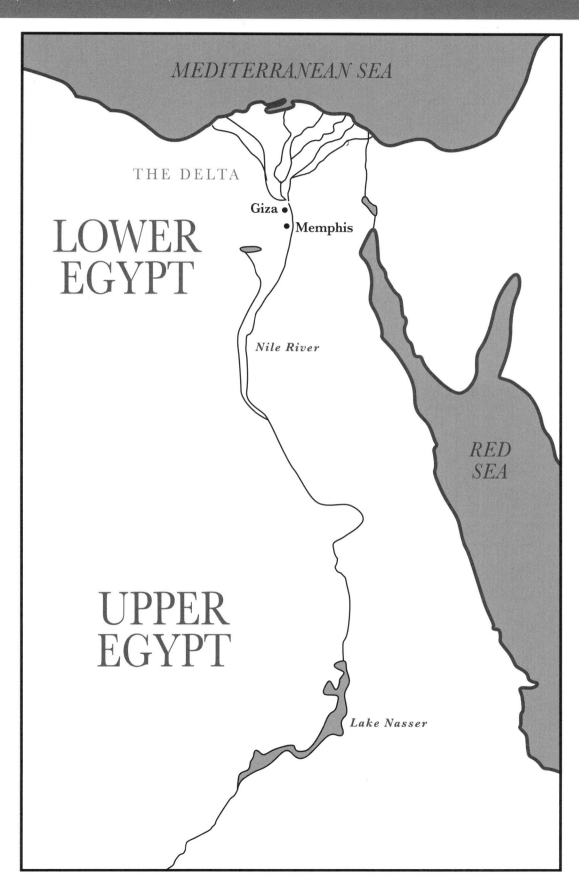

STEP 1: Draw a straight line up and down. Mark 1/4 and 1/2 of the line. Draw an oval on the top 1/4 section for the sarcophagus headdress.

STEP 2: Draw another oval that reaches from the middle of your first oval to the bottom of your line marking 1/2. Add a smaller oval at the bottom of your straight line.

STEP 3: Erase your middle line. Draw a smaller oval for the head. Add lines to connect the large oval and bottom circle.

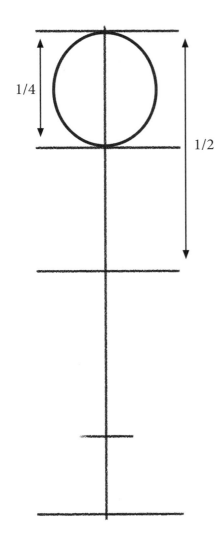
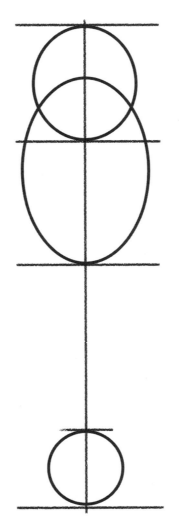
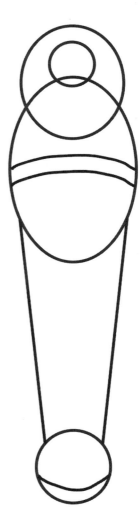

STEP 4: Add ears, facial features, a neck, and hands. Shape the headdress a little more.

STEP 5: Erase the unnecessary lines (shown in gray). Square off the feet a little more.

STEP 6: Make an X shape above the hands and then add the hook and flail. Decorate and color your sarcophagus however you want!

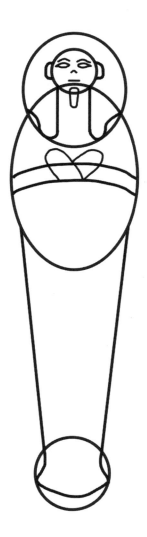
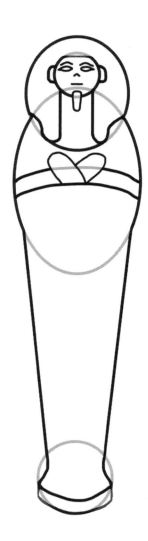
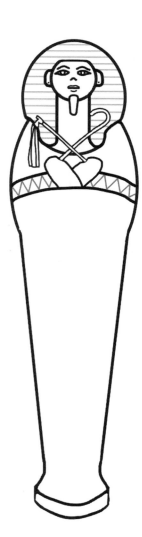

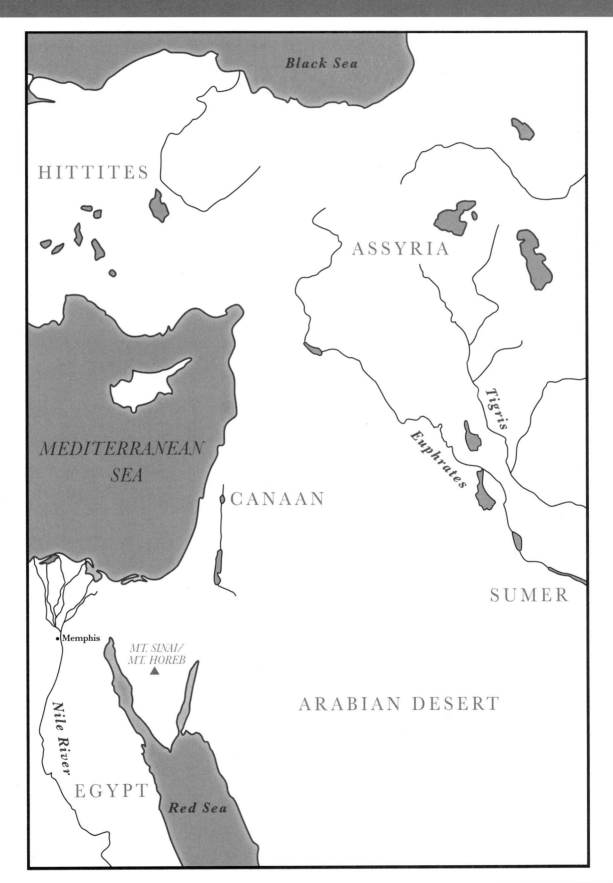

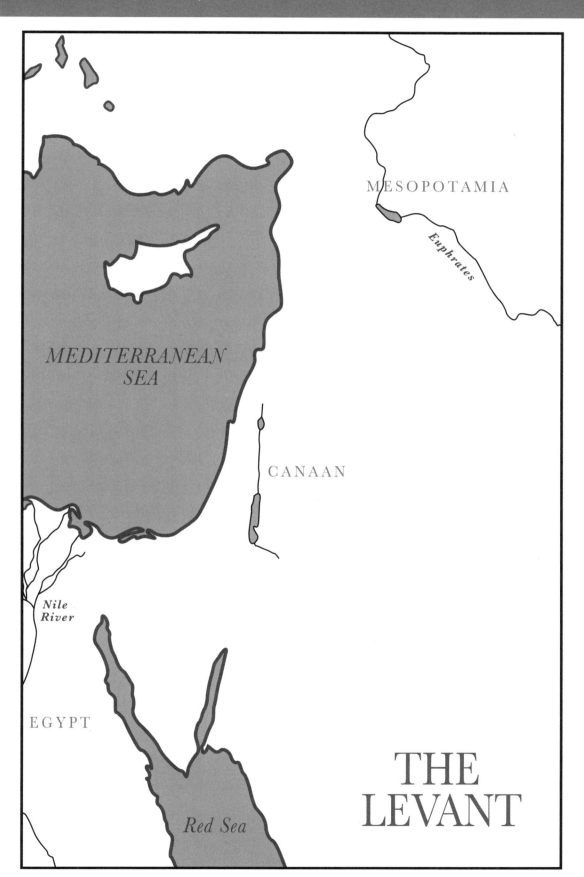

MESOPOTAMIA

Euphrates

MEDITERRANEAN
SEA

CANAAN

Nile
River

EGYPT

THE
LEVANT

Red Sea

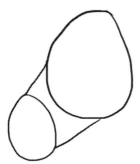

STEP 1: Draw two circles as shown to the left and then draw two lines connecting them. Your circles do not need to be perfect.

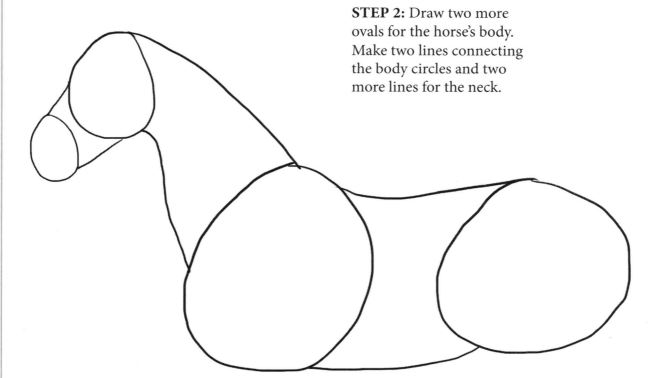

STEP 2: Draw two more ovals for the horse's body. Make two lines connecting the body circles and two more lines for the neck.

STEP 3: Draw 4 circles for the
horse's hooves, and just above
each hoof draw an additional
smaller circle for the ankles. Connect the body with the hooves as
shown below.

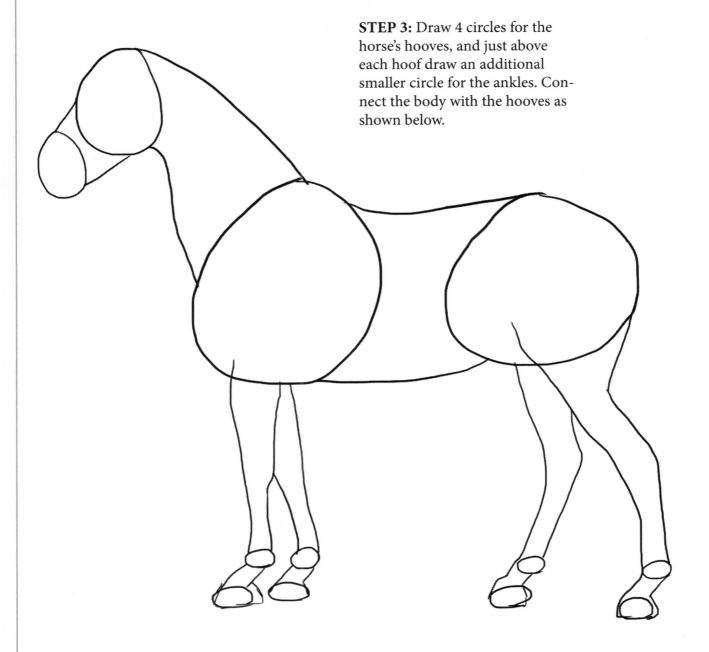

STEP 4: Add details: eyes, ears, mouth, mane, and tail. Erase your unnecessary guide lines. Take this opportunity to smooth out any mistakes. Color your horse and enjoy!

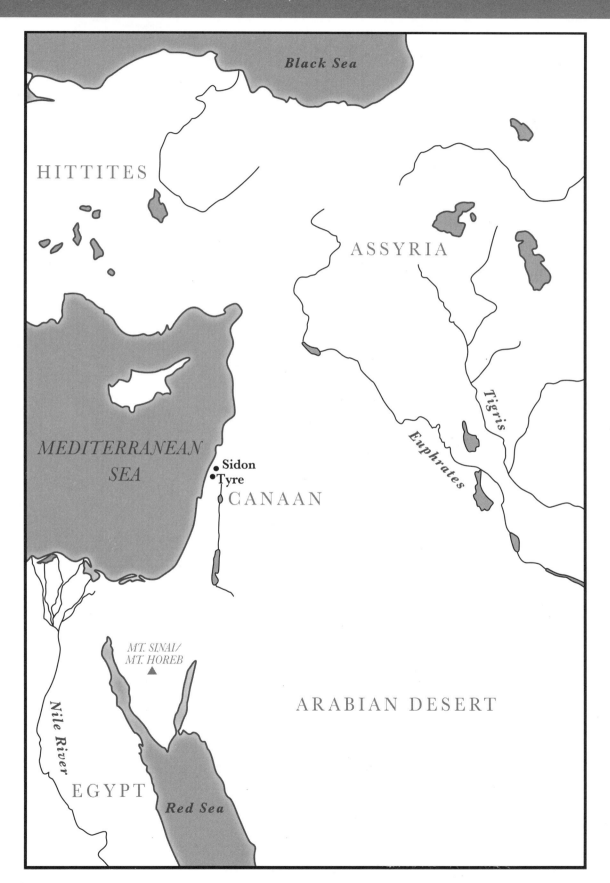

Across

4. Very hilly territory that was an important trade route
6. Dwelt in the cities of Tyre and Sidon
8. As the Hittites pushed south, they battled this empire

Down

1. Where the Hittites settled around 2000 B.C.
2. The Canaanites grazed these in their grassy fields
3. Strip of land connecting Egypt and Mesopotamia
4. The Phoenicians were famous for these trees
5. The greatest gift of Phoenicia
7. A rugged, mountain-dwelling folk

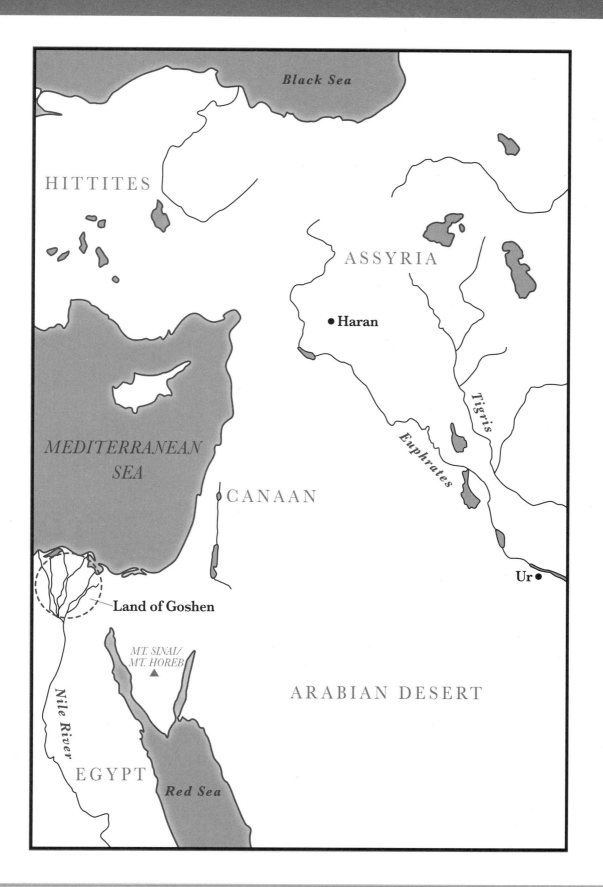

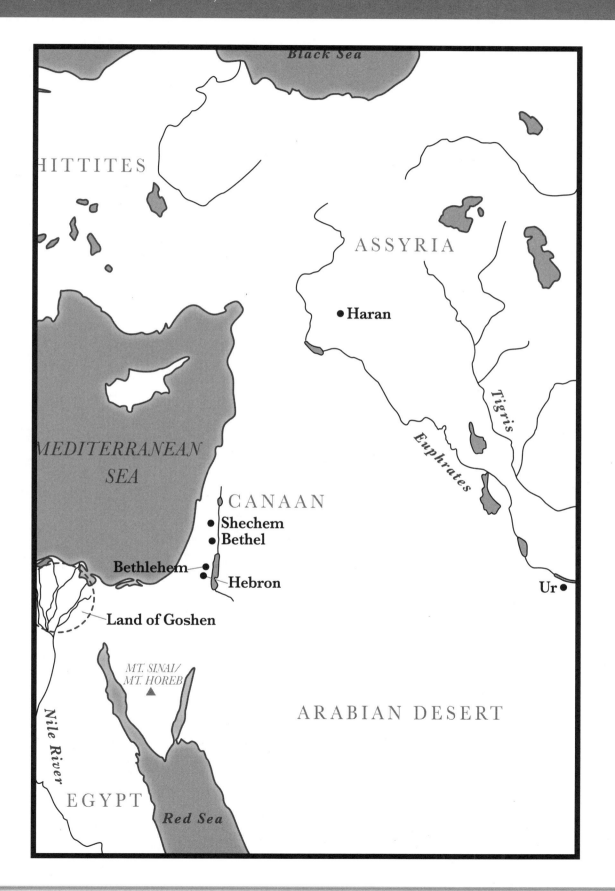

STEP 1: Draw a stick figure with one arm raised.

STEP 2: Draw clothes on your stick figure.

STEP 3: Add Moses' eyes, nose and mustache. Draw ovals for his hands and draw a straight line through his hand where his staff should go. Make ovals for his feet.

STEP 4: Add Moses' beard. Add more details to his hands and staff.

STEP 5: Add more details to his hands, clothes, etc. Color your drawing and enjoy!

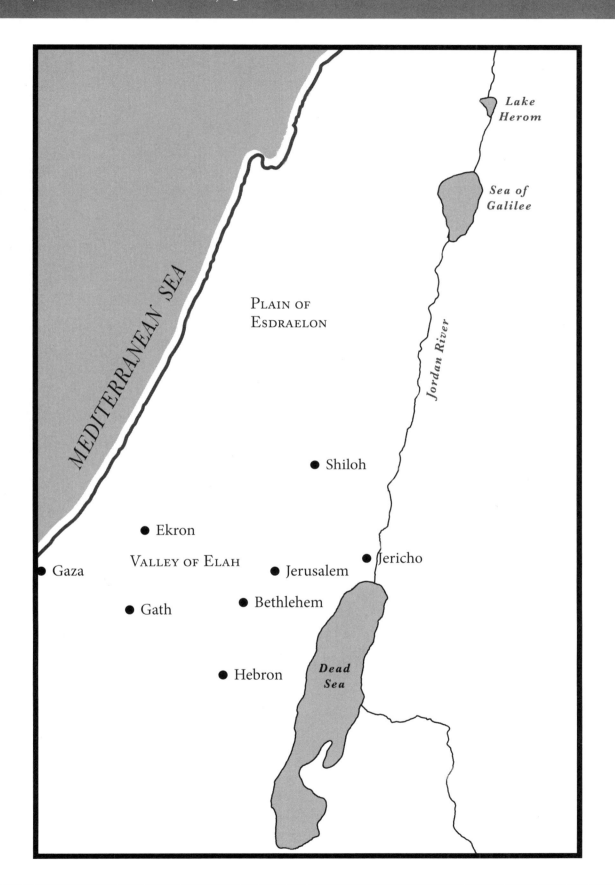

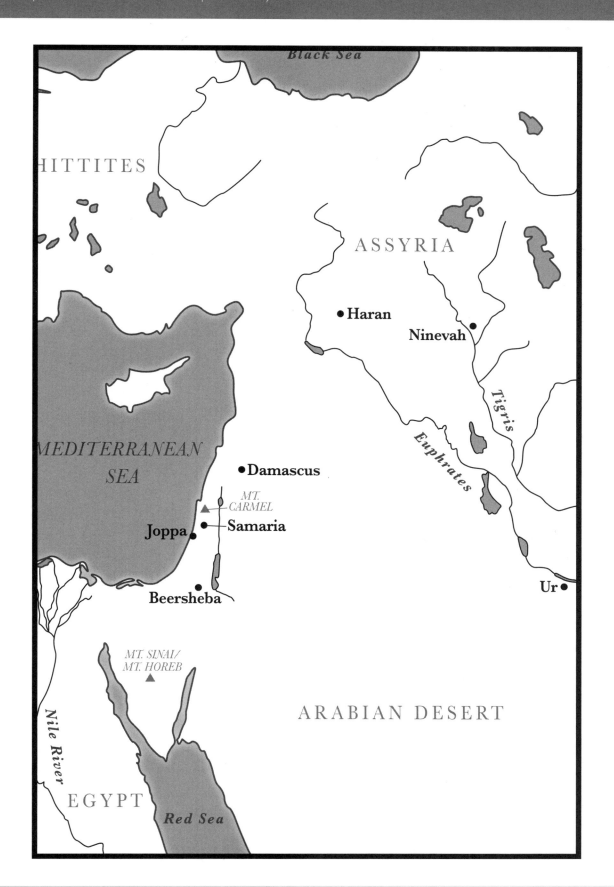

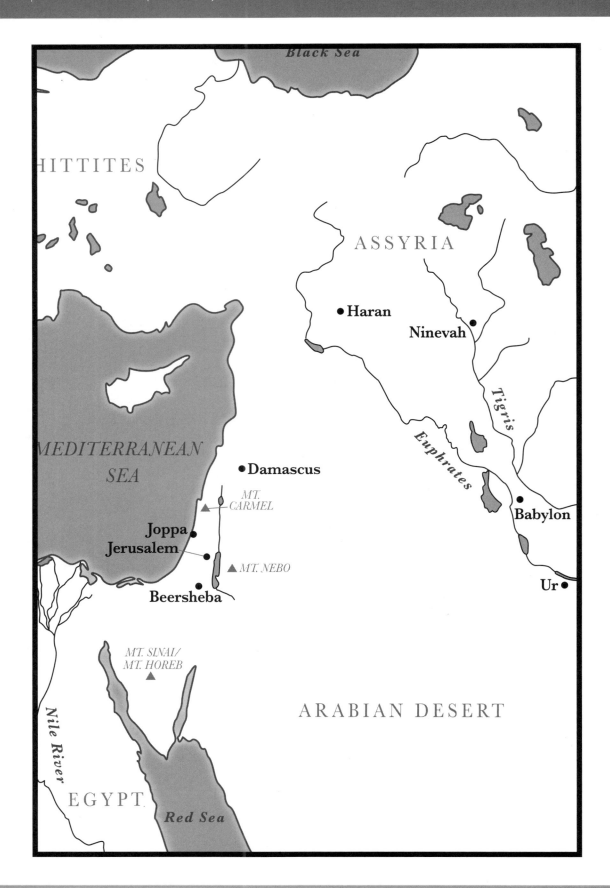

The Splendor of Babylon Word Search Clues

1. The leader of those who overthrew Assyria was a man named _____.
2. The lands of the Assyrians now became _____ of Babylon, meaning that they owed allegiance and paid tribute to Babylon.
3. Nabopolassar made _____ an important city once again.
4. The country overthrown by Nabopolassar was _____.
5. _____ had the wisdom of the father and the might of the son.
6. After the fall of Assyria, the Egyptians were again trying to win back their old territories in the _____.
7. The little kingdom of _____ gave Nebuchadnezzar trouble.
8. The prophet Jeremiah warned King _____ that God had given Nebuchadnezzar power and that a rebellion was ill advised.
9. Nebuchadnezzar married the Median princess _____.
10. Nebuchadnezzar loved his wife and in order to ease her homesickness, he created the Hanging _____ of Babylon.
11. This terraced pyramid with exotic plants imported from Media is now called one of the _____ of the world.
12. Nebuchadnezzar had wall built to surround the city that were so thick that two ____ could ride side by side on them.
13. The gates of Babylon were painted blue and decorated with royal _____.
14. Nebuchadnezzar also wanted to rebuild the great _____ of the Sumerian period.
15. The _____ River flowed right through the city of Babylon.
16. _____, the last king of Babylon, was foolish enough to throw a party while the city was under attack.

The Splendor of Babylon Word Search

```
N A S S Y R I A W B N S N V K
P E Z E Y A G S E Y T O A A F
B P B F T H C L W O H G B S B
Y A B U A A S W I Q A S O S O
D W B D C H R R Z R I I P A R
T P U Y A H A H D O K T O L B
L J Z Z L H A E P Z E Y L S F
Z V Z L C O N D W U D M A C O
L A Y C B S N T N P E A S R I
R D C B A B X J N E Z H S C P
S T A R U G G I Z A Z C A P S
J G G V A L F G R V V Z R I O
H T J Y R D Y R T P Z E A L V
H E G O T Z J S A L Q K L R Z
L I O N S V W S R E D N O W O
```

Note: Some words may appear backwards. If you have trouble figuring out the words from your clues, see if you can find the words from this list: Amytis, Assyria, Babylon, Belshazzar, Chariots, Euphrates, Gardens, Judah, Levant, Lions, Nabopolassar, Nebuchadnezzar, Vassals, Wonders, Zedekiah, Ziggurats

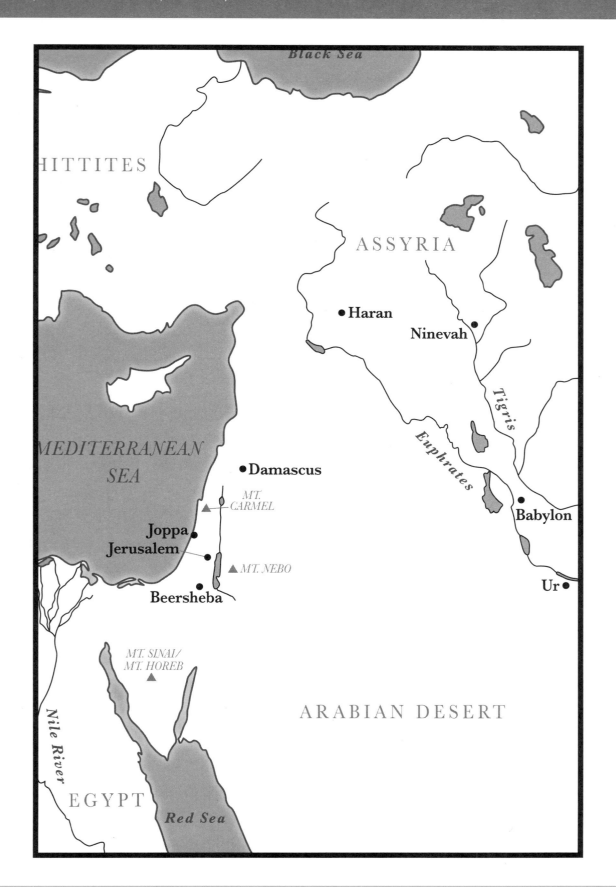

START

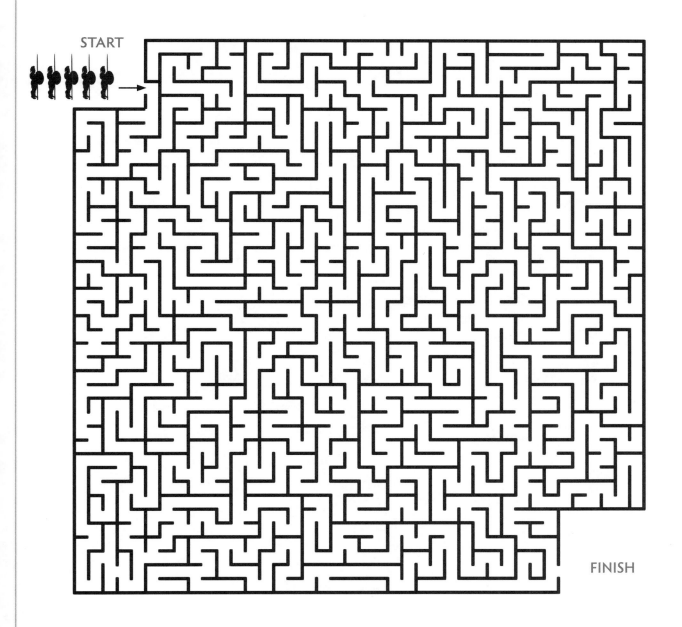

FINISH

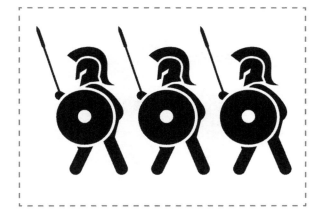

MACEDONIA

MT. OLYMPUS ▲

GREECE

• Troy

Aegan Sea

Delphi
•

Thebes
•

Athens
•

Miletus
•

Corinth •

Mycenae •

Sparta
•

Sea of Crete

Knossos
•

CRETE

MEDITERRANEAN SEA

Across

3. Common animal depicted in frescoes.
4. Name given by Evans to the ancient people of Crete.
8. Half-man, half-bull.
9. Legendary king of Crete.
10. Glorious city ruins were discovered in.

Down

1. Many of these can be found in the Mediterranean.
2. Paintings done on plaster walls or ceilings.
4. Thought of as the end of the world.
5. Archaeologist who uncovered the ruins of Crete
6. Greek poet who described Crete
7. "A land in the midst of a wine-dark sea."

MACEDONIA

MT. OLYMPUS ▲

GREECE

Troy •

Aegan Sea

Delphi
•

Thebes
Athens

Corinth •

Mycenae •

Sparta
•

Miletus
•

Sea of Crete

Knossos
•

CRETE

MEDITERRANEAN SEA

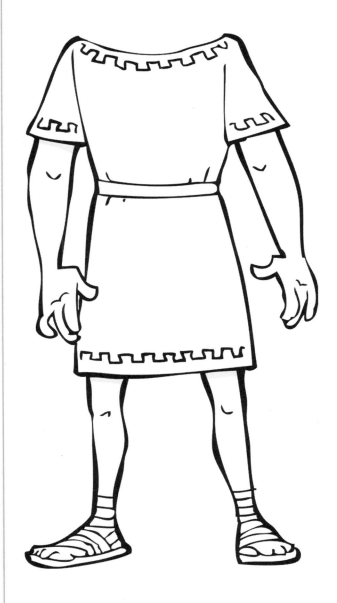

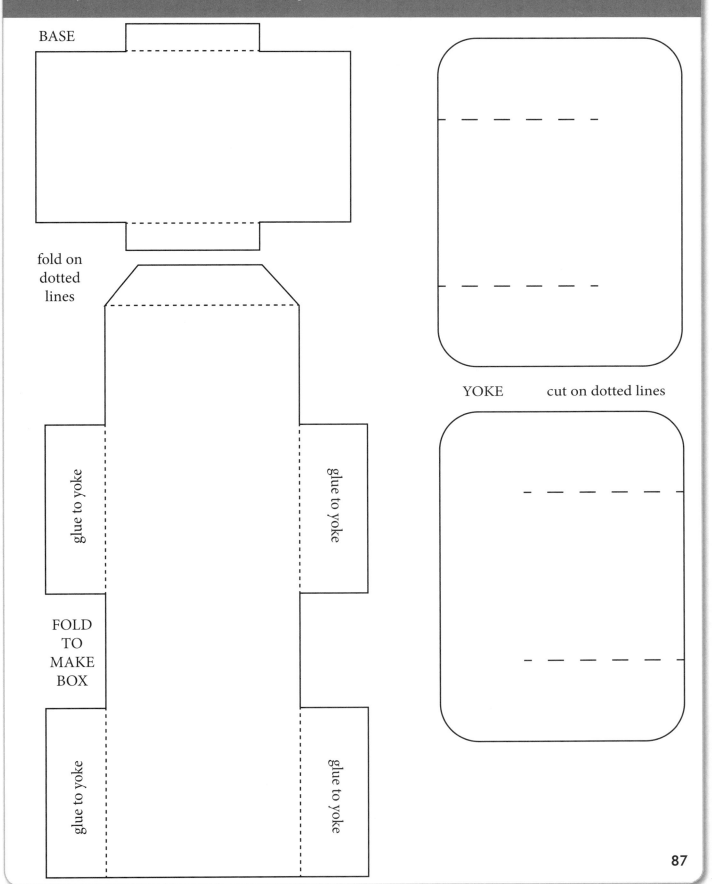

BASE

fold on
dotted
lines

glue to yoke

glue to yoke

FOLD
TO
MAKE
BOX

glue to yoke

glue to yoke

YOKE   cut on dotted lines

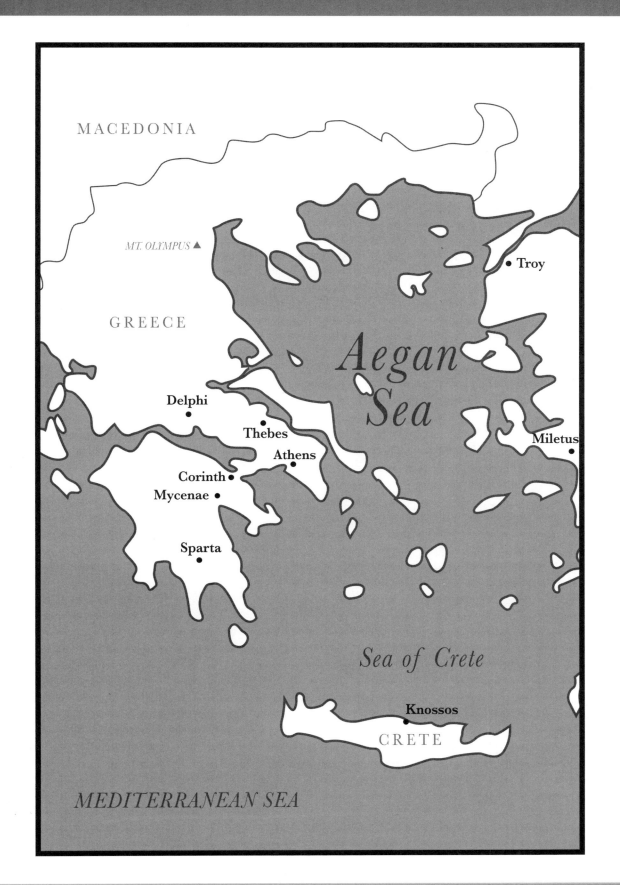

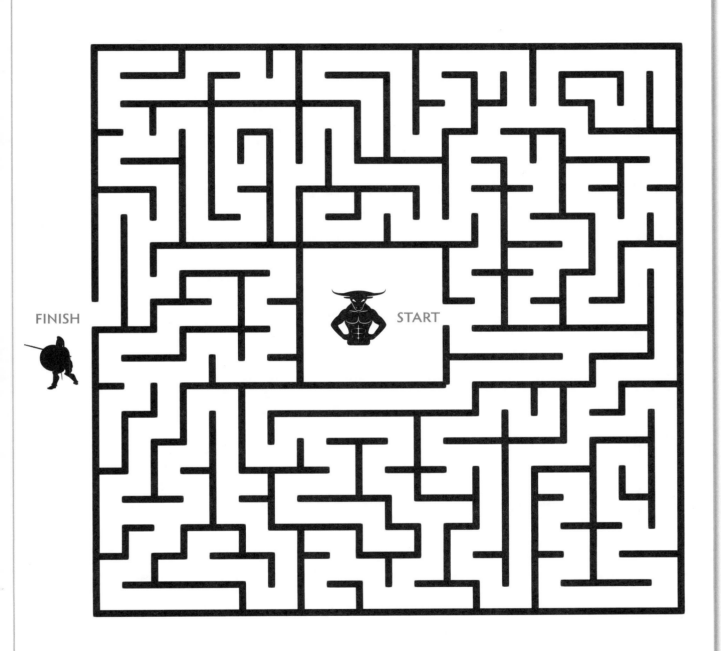

FINISH

START

MACEDONIA

MT. OLYMPUS ▲

GREECE

*Aegan
Sea*

Troy

Delphi

Thebes

Athens

Miletus

Corinth

Mycenae

Sparta

Sea of Crete

Knossos

CRETE

MEDITERRANEAN SEA

The Cradle of Democracy Word Search Clues

1. Means "rule by king."
2. The Greek city was called the _____.
3. The polis was essentially its own little _____.
4. A government where a people governs itself is called a _____.
5. Laws were changed to reduce the power of the kings and give more to the _____.
6. In Athens, the elected leaders were called _____.
7. In Athens, _____ believed that laws would work best if there were very harsh punishments for breaking them.
8. _____ agreed to write a new set of laws for Athens. He ended the power of the rich over the poor by allowing all citizens to serve in an assembly that governed the city.
9. Greeks turned to wise men and asked them to write _____ for their cities.
10. The laws of _____ valued equality, military power, and simple living.
11. Military training of Spartan boys from the age of 7 to 29.
12. Spartan wives told their husbands to come back with their _____ or on it.
13. A person who seized power by force and ruled alone without an assembly or the participation of the citizens.

The Cradle of Democracy Word Search

```
Y  S  G  K  P  N  T  Z  P  G  O  R  N  T  I
W  C  I  L  O  O  A  S  T  N  A  R  Y  T  V
Q  P  A  L  A  Z  W  P  W  D  B  U  W  F  Y
C  I  O  R  O  W  O  A  N  M  G  K  D  K  L
B  S  U  U  C  P  S  R  L  X  Y  Y  R  E  D
M  R  S  C  Y  O  J  T  K  T  H  O  B  A  S
L  K  F  S  W  G  M  A  I  L  C  C  M  Z  S
B  W  J  G  Q  P  P  E  G  P  R  A  P  D  U
Y  G  G  E  P  U  E  L  D  M  A  R  Q  Q  C
A  R  C  H  O  N  S  O  O  R  N  D  P  S  R
G  O  C  D  D  I  S  D  P  O  O  D  H  R  C
J  F  I  S  M  L  G  A  Q  L  M  I  U  J  Y
A  I  X  D  I  N  A  L  G  C  E  K  C  Q  Z
C  M  N  T  I  W  O  Z  I  L  J  P  Q  B  L
V  Z  M  K  F  S  V  J  D  A  G  O  G  E  K
```

Note: Some words may appear backwards. If you have trouble figuring out the words from your clues, see if you can find the words from this list: Agoge, Archons, Democracy, Draco, Kingdom, Laws, Monarchy, People, Polis, Shield, Solon, Sparta, Tyrant

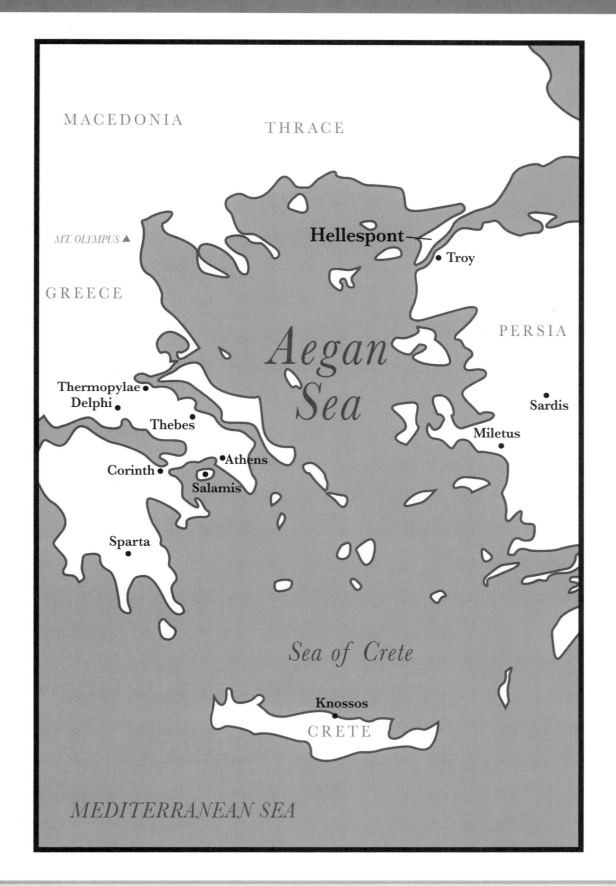

MACEDONIA   THRACE

MT. OLYMPUS ▲

GREECE

Hellespont

• **Troy**

Aegan Sea

PERSIA

Thermopylae •
Delphi •

Sardis

Thebes •

Miletus

• **Athens**

Corinth •
Salamis

Sparta •

Sea of Crete

Knossos •

CRETE

MEDITERRANEAN SEA

XESEXR

☐☐☐☐☐☐
　　　3　　11

RAEPIS

☐☐☐☐☐☐
　　　5

SAIANORMI

☐☐☐☐☐　☐☐☐☐☐
　　　　　　　　8

GEERK ELGAUE

☐☐☐☐☐☐　☐☐☐☐☐☐
　　　　　　　10

SATRAPN MYAR

☐☐☐☐☐☐☐　☐☐☐☐
　　　　　　　　4

INHNATA VNYA

☐☐☐☐☐☐☐☐　☐☐☐☐
　　　2

COKBL TEH NSU

☐☐☐☐☐☐　☐☐☐☐　☐☐☐
　　　9　　　　　　　6

LERMYTAPHEO

☐☐☐☐☐☐☐☐☐☐☐
　7

TARSIGHT FO MASASLI

☐☐☐☐☐☐☐☐☐　☐☐
　1

☐☐☐☐☐☐☐
　　　　　　12

☐☐☐☐☐☐☐☐☐☐☐☐
1　2　3　4　5　6　7　8　9　10　11　12

Who won the war for the Greeks but ultimately ended up exiled because of his pride?

STEP 1: Using a ruler, draw two straight lines.

STEP 2: Connect the lines on the right-hand side of your boat with a curved line. On the left hand side of the top line, draw a curved line with a circle.

STEP 3: Connect the lines as shown, add details to the back side of the boat.

STEP 4: Add a long, slightly curved line on the front of your boat. Draw two more straight lines using a ruler.

STEP 5: Add some circles which will be the holes from which the oars extend from.

STEP 6: Add two more smaller lines extending from the oar level. Connect the top line with your new line. Add two lines to form the bottom of the boat on the back and front.

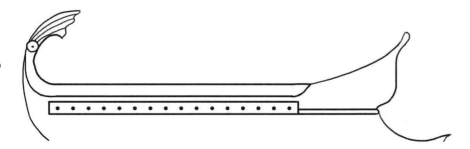

STEP 7: Using a ruler, draw angled lines for your oars. They should all be at the same angle.

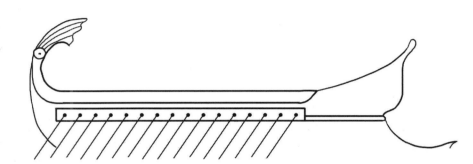

STEP 8: Add waves.

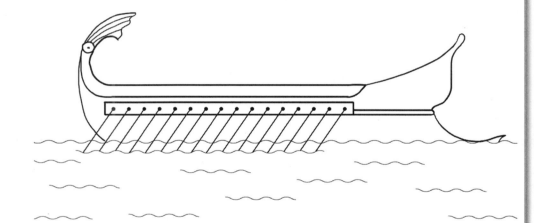

STEP 9: Add your mast and sail. Color and decorate your Greek warship however you like! Enjoy!

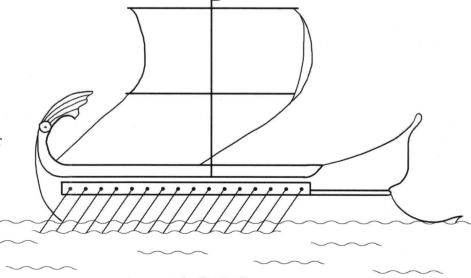

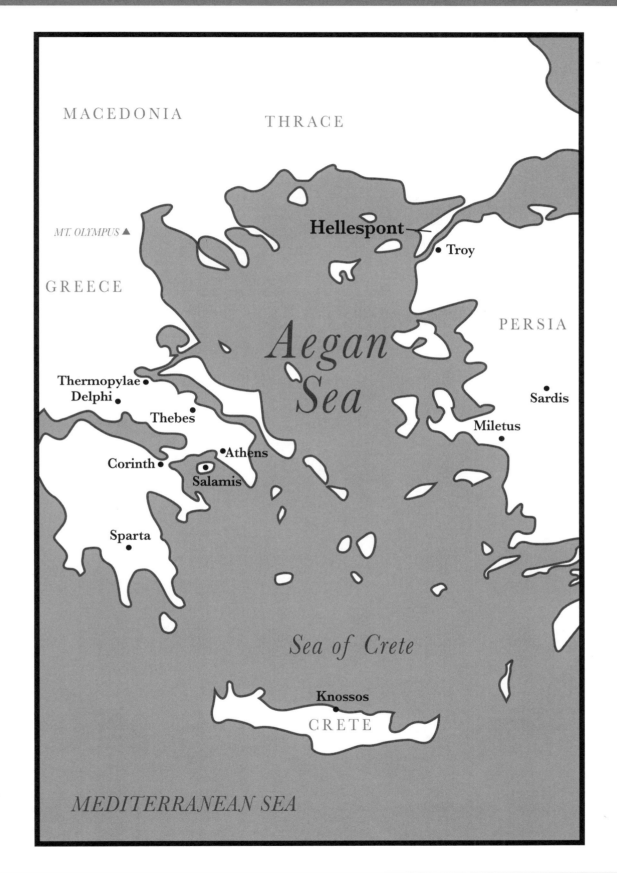

Socrates Spoon Person Template

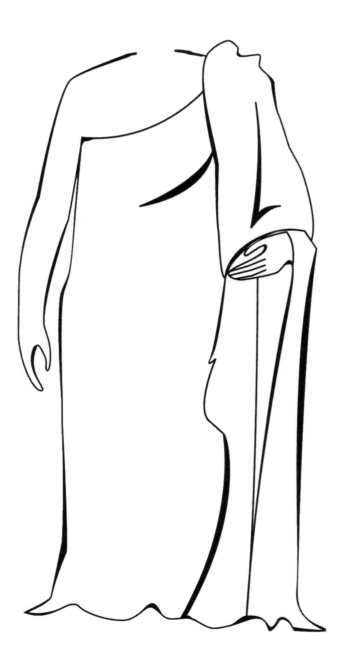

Plato Spoon Person Template

PERFECT
IDEA

Aristotle Spoon Person Template

"WE ARE WHAT WE REPEATEDLY DO. EXCELLENCE, THEN, IS NOT AN ACT, BUT A HABIT."

"HAPPINESS DEPENDS UPON OURSELVES."

"MEMORY IS THE SCRIBE OF THE SOUL."

"IT IS THE MARK OF AN EDUCATED MIND TO BE ABLE TO ENTERTAIN A THOUGHT WITHOUT ACCEPTING IT."

"THE WORST FORM OF INEQUALITY IS TO TRY TO MAKE UNEQUAL THINGS EQUAL."

"HOPE IS A WAKING DREAM."

"PLEASURE IN THE JOB PUTS PERFECTION IN THE WORK."

"THE ENERGY OF THE MIND IS THE ESSENCE OF LIFE."

"WICKED MEN OBEY FROM FEAR; GOOD MEN, FROM LOVE."

"THE EDUCATED DIFFER FROM THE UNEDUCATED AS MUCH AS THE LIVING FROM THE DEAD."

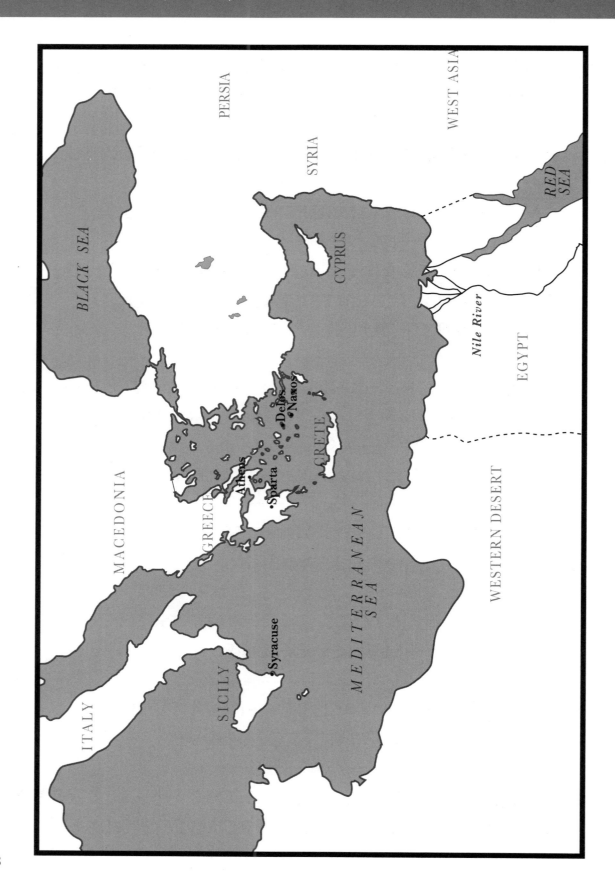

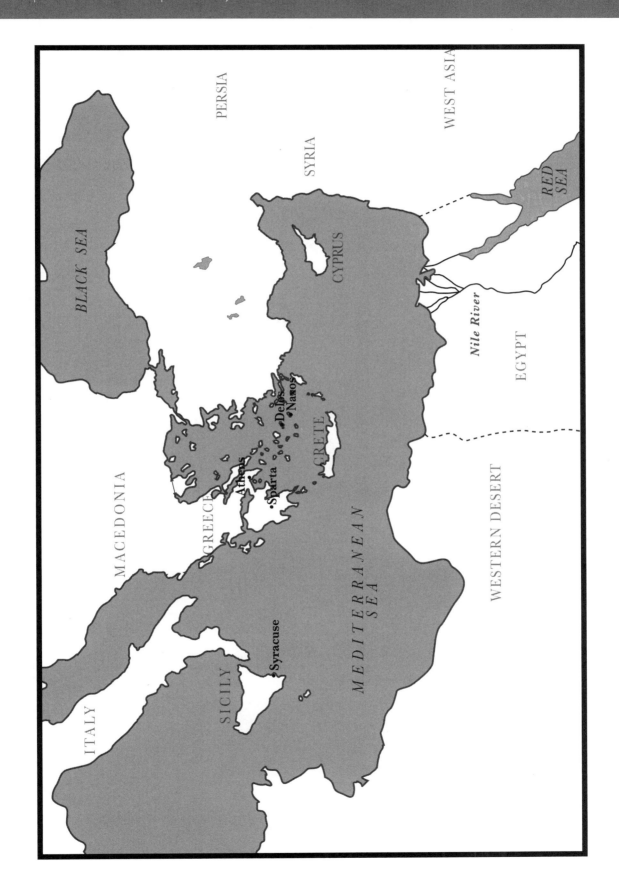

Chapter 19   Cryptogram   **TO WHOM DO YOU LEAVE YOUR EMPIRE?**

A	B	C	D	E	F	G	H	I	J	K	L	M	N	O	P	Q	R	S	T	U	V	W	X	Y	Z
8				24						3			17						14					4	

___ ___   ___ ___ ___   ___ ___ ___ ___ ___ ___ ___ ___ ___
14 26   14 1 24   2 14 19 26 17 21 24 2 14

Alexander said this to his generals when they asked who he would leave his empire to.

After cracking the code and filling in your answer, you should have a numeric symbol for twelve letters. Fill in a numeric symbol for the remaining letters of your own choosing and then write out a short coded message to your mom or dad below (you may want to use a scrap sheet of paper to practice your coded message). Give it to your parents for them to decipher.

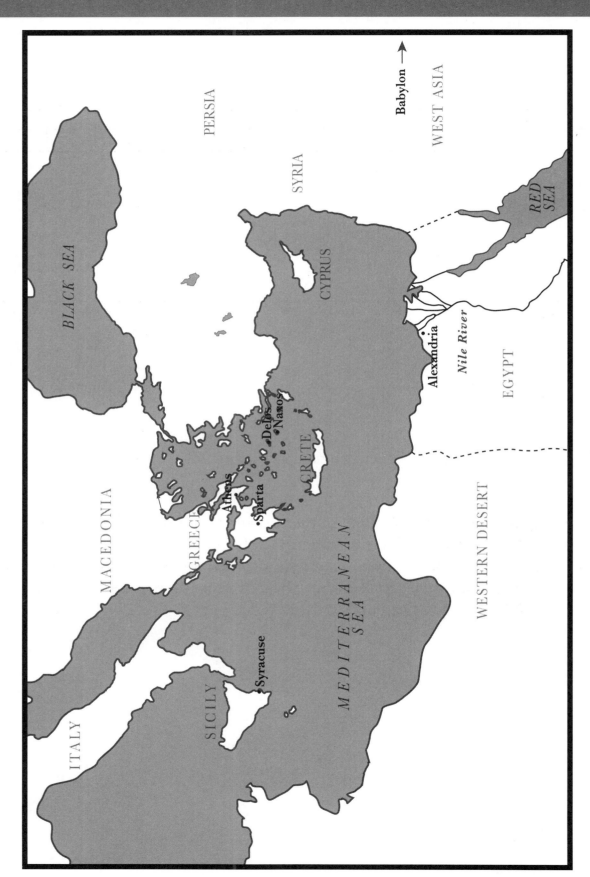

START

FINISH

MOLTYPE

☐☐☐☐☐☐☐
    10

DOL TSTENTEMA

☐☐☐   ☐☐☐☐☐☐☐☐☐
                6

WEERBH

☐☐☐☐☐☐

NIOTARALSTN

☐☐☐☐☐☐☐☐☐☐
  4

REGKE

☐☐☐☐☐

NETVEYS SISBERC

☐☐☐☐☐☐☐   ☐☐☐☐☐☐☐
              1

DOEGUNN

☐☐☐☐☐☐☐
      9

WIINTRG SDKE

☐☐☐☐☐☐☐   ☐☐☐☐
      7

RPPUSAY LRSCLO

☐☐☐☐☐☐☐   ☐☐☐☐☐
  3

LILQU

☐☐☐☐☐
  5   8

EDTIICANL

☐☐☐☐☐☐☐☐☐
      2

☐☐☐☐☐☐☐☐☐☐
1 2 3 4 5 6 7 8 9 10

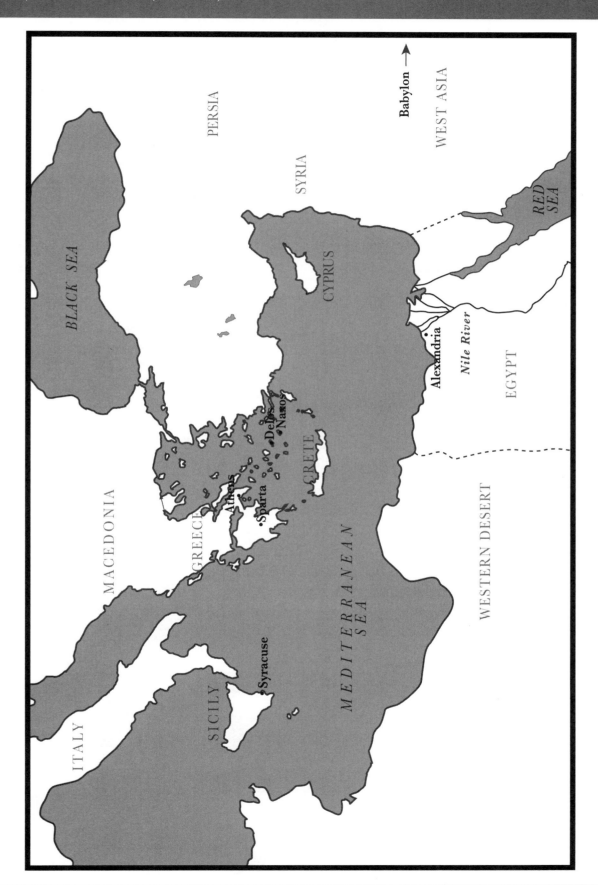

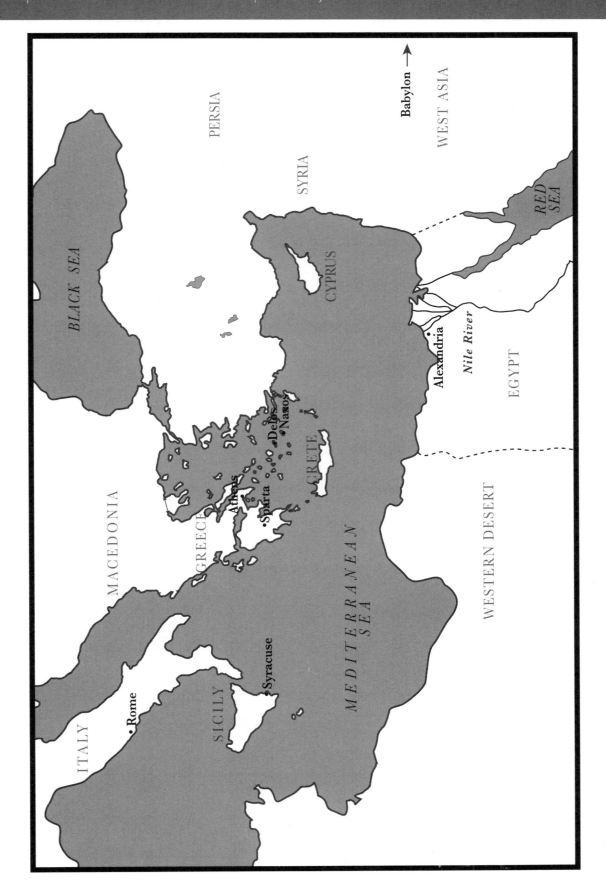

START

FINISH

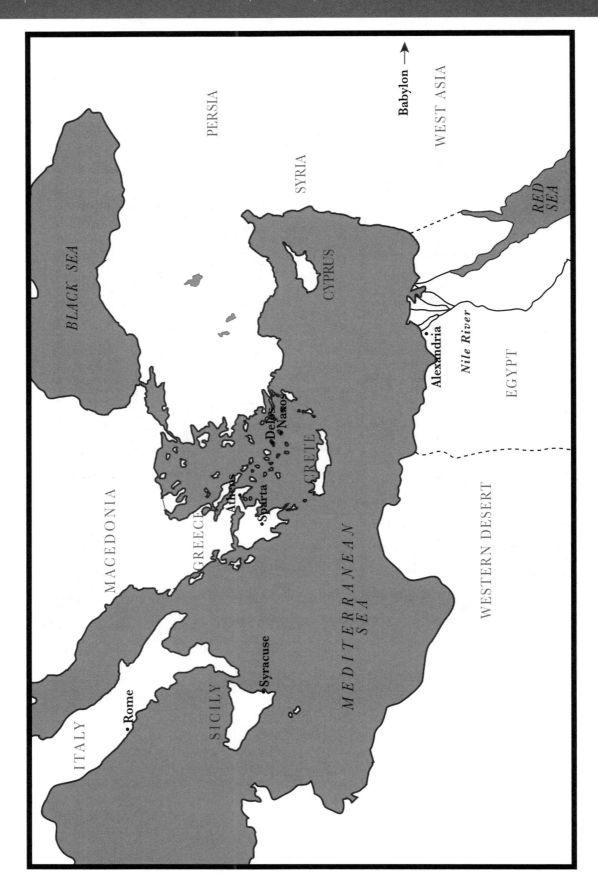

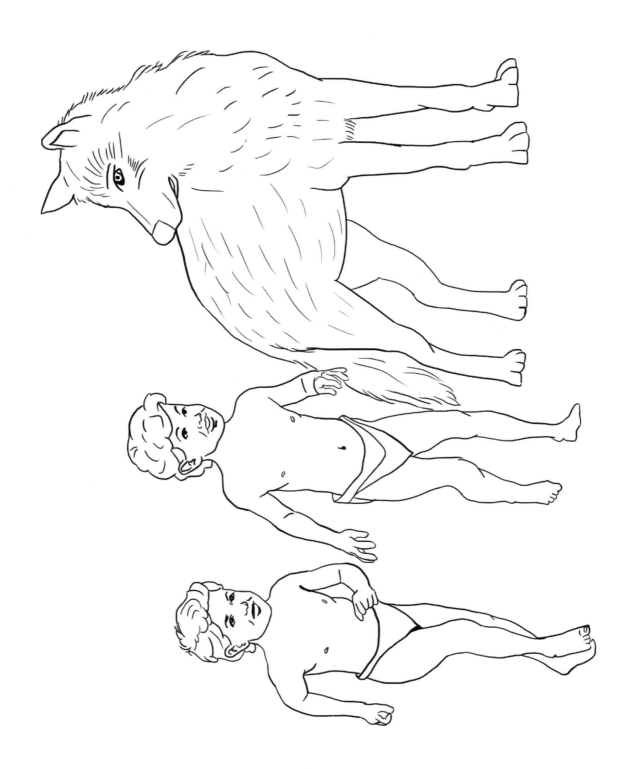

TENNOMERGV

⬜⬜⬜⬜⬜⬜⬜⬜⬜⬜
　　　　　　1

TEEDELC

⬜⬜⬜⬜⬜⬜⬜
　　8

SIFLFIOCA

⬜⬜⬜⬜⬜⬜⬜⬜⬜
　　　　7

PEELOP VEORGN

⬜⬜⬜⬜⬜⬜　⬜⬜⬜⬜⬜⬜
　　　3

REUL FO WSAL

⬜⬜⬜⬜　⬜⬜　⬜⬜⬜⬜
　　　2

TOW SOCSULN

⬜⬜⬜　⬜⬜⬜⬜⬜⬜⬜
　　　　　　　4

TESNEA

⬜⬜⬜⬜⬜⬜
　　

LIBSAESEMS

⬜⬜⬜⬜⬜⬜⬜⬜⬜⬜
　　　　　5

DESLIAE

⬜⬜⬜⬜⬜⬜⬜
　　　6

⬜⬜⬜⬜⬜⬜⬜⬜
1　2　3　4　5　6　7　8

STEP 1: Draw an angled circle as shown.

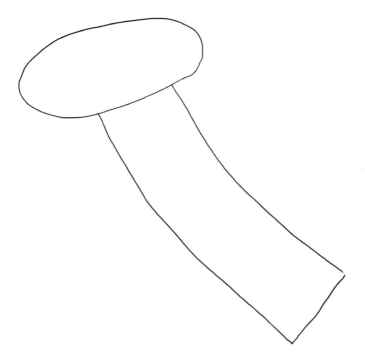

STEP 2: Add two slightly curved angled lines, and draw a line to connect them.

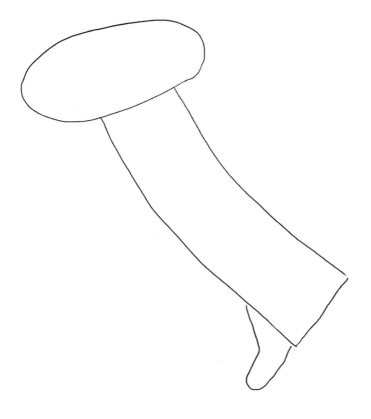

STEP 3: Add the "toe" of the boot of italy.

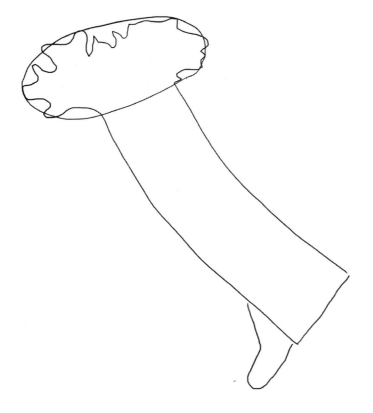

STEP 4: Start adding land detail at the top. Use a map of Italy as your guide. It doesn't have to be perfect.

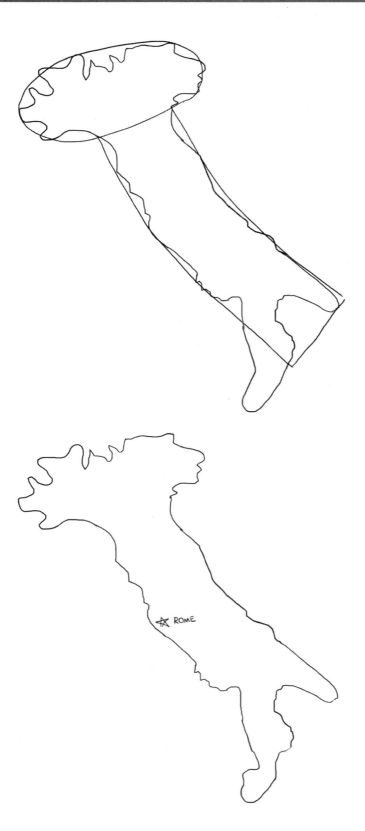

STEP 3: Continue your land details.

STEP 4: Once you have finished your land details, erase your guide lines. Add a star where Rome should be and label it. Color and deorate Italy. Enjoy!

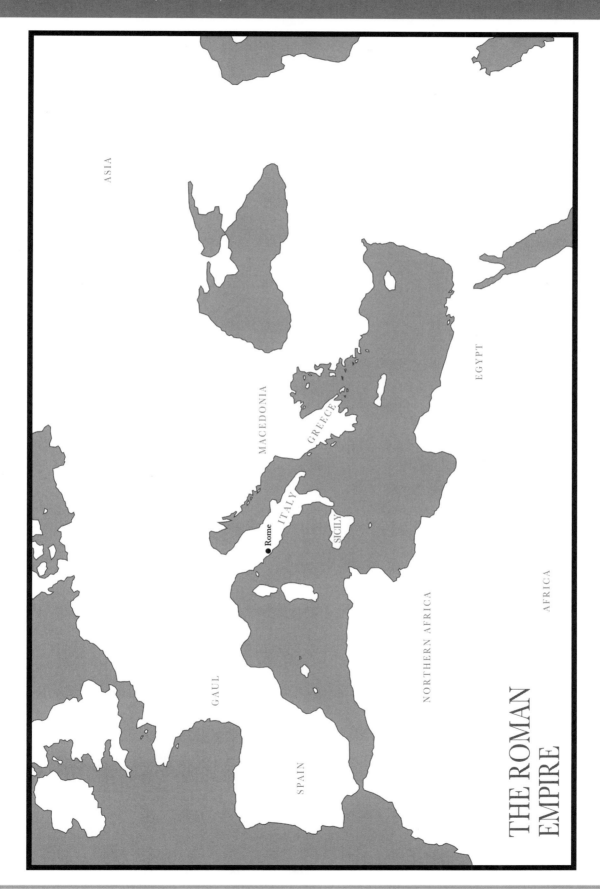

ASIA

MACEDONIA

GREECE

EGYPT

ITALY

SICILY

Rome

NORTHERN AFRICA

AFRICA

GAUL

SPAIN

THE ROMAN
EMPIRE

ROME

STEP 1: Draw the island of
Sicily on your map of Italy.

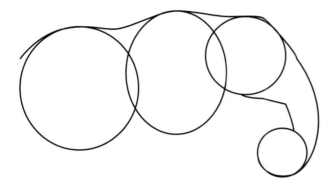

STEP 1: Draw three overlapping circles as shown. Add a smaller circle for the end of your elephant's trunk. Connect the circles with lines for its trunk and mouth.

STEP 2: Add your elephant's back legs. Connect the legs with one smooth line going up to the neck. Start adding more details to the mouth and trunk.

STEP 3: Add the front legs. Draw circles for the ankle and knee joints to make drawing them easier. Add tusks.

STEP 4: Finish with some details around the mouth. Add eyes and a tail.

STEP 5: Now customize your elephant. Add a saddle, armor, shields, or a place for soldiers to ride. Make sure your elephant is ready for battle! Color and enjoy!

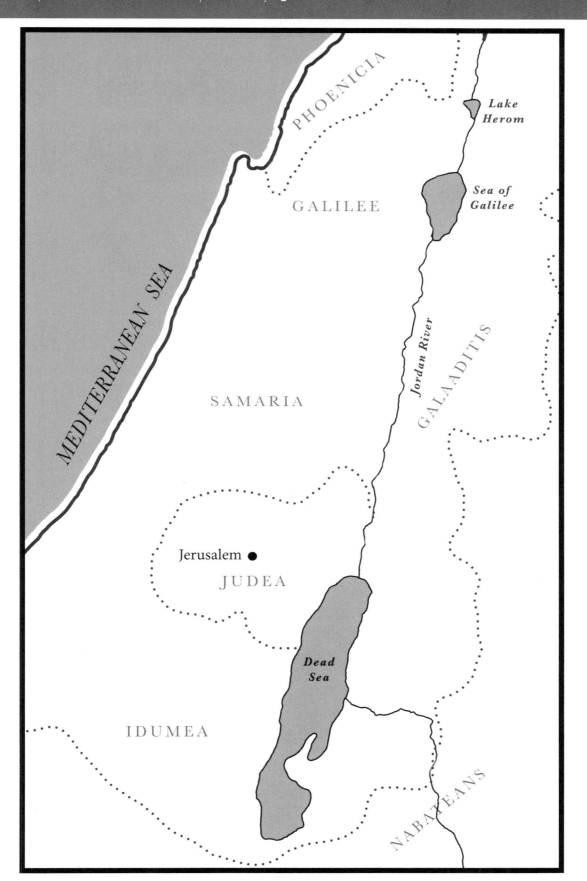

PHOENICIA

Lake
Herom

Sea of
Galilee

GALILEE

MEDITERRANEAN SEA

Jordan River

GALAADITIS

SAMARIA

Jerusalem ●

JUDEA

Dead
Sea

IDUMEA

NABATEANS

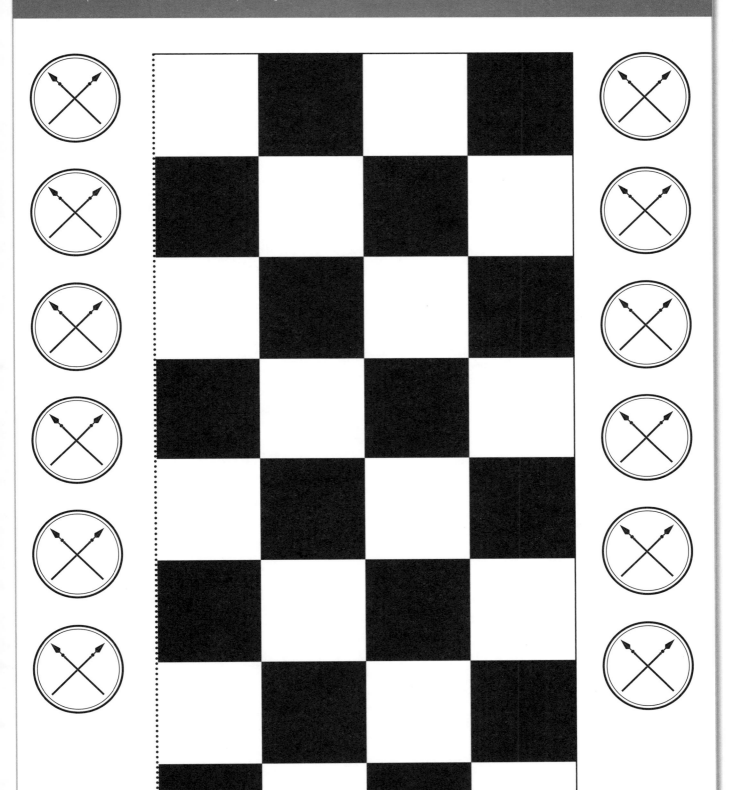

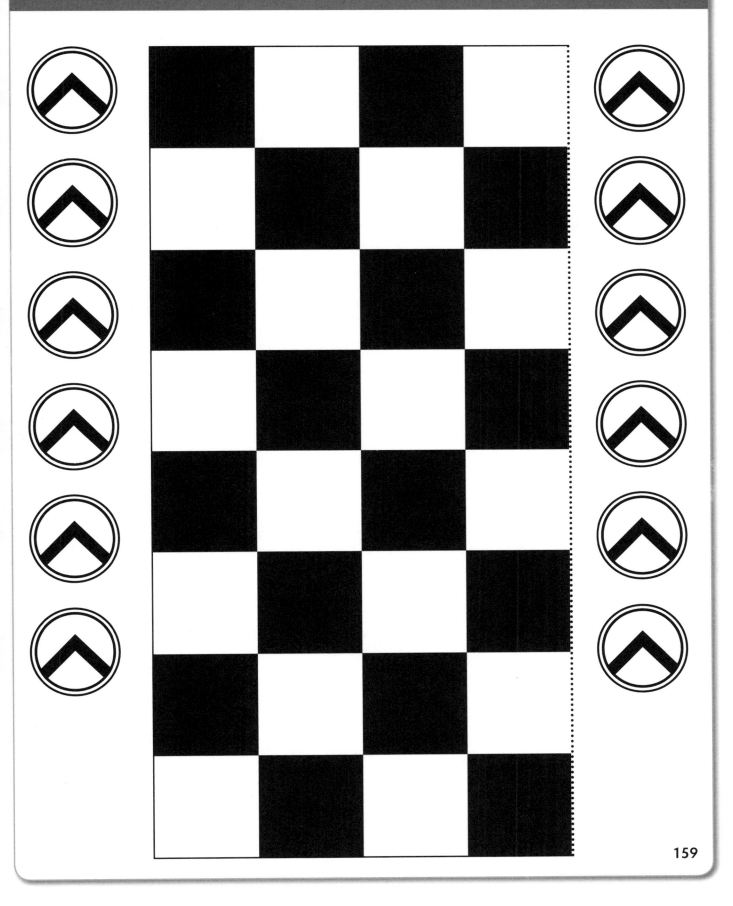

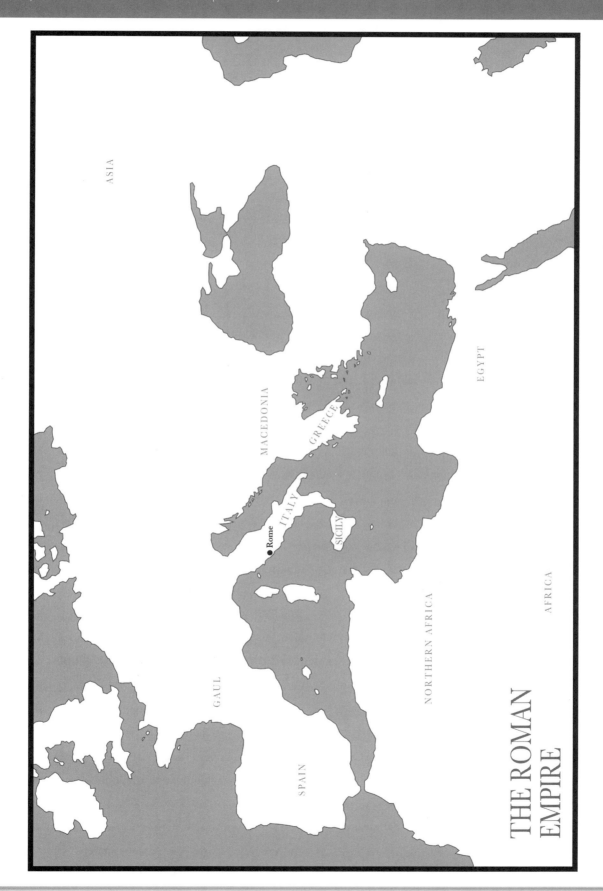

ASIA

MACEDONIA

GREECE

EGYPT

ITALY

SICILY

● Rome

GAUL

NORTHERN AFRICA

AFRICA

SPAIN

THE ROMAN
EMPIRE

STEP 1: Draw a hook shape as shown. We are starting with the eagle's brow.

STEP 2: Attach two more curved lines as shown, beginning the shape of the beak.

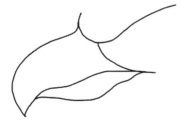

STEP 3: Finish drawing out the beak by adding two more lines.

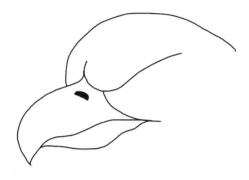

STEP 4: Make a large curved line for the top of the eagle's head. Draw and fill in the eagle's nostril on its beak.

STEP 5: Continue the line of the top of the eagle's head, but make feather shapes the rest of the way down. Add another layer of feathers if you like.

STEP 6: Make two circles for the eagle's eyes. Add as many details as you like, color and enjoy!

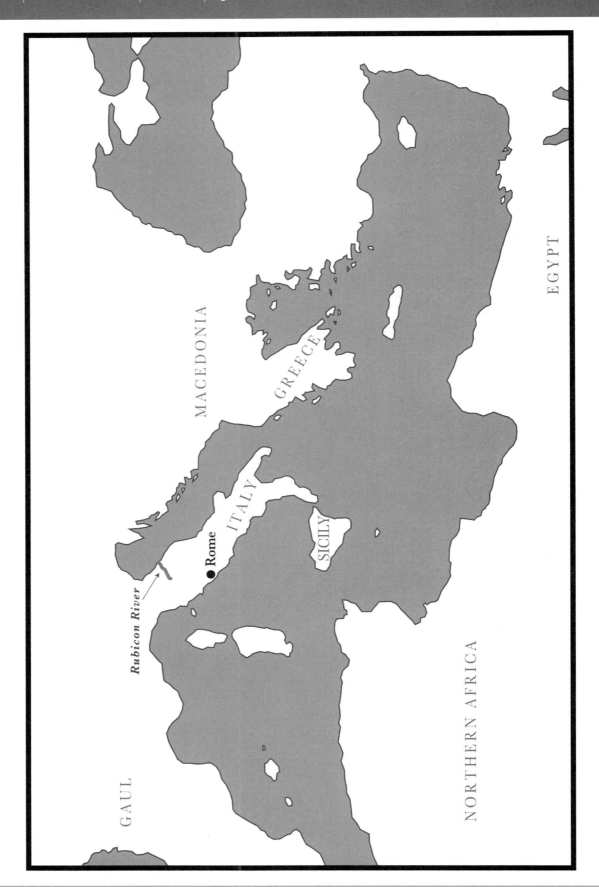

Across

4. Caesar gave _____ to the supporters of Pompey.
5. _____ had Pompey stabbed to death.
6. Caesar's most trusted friend.
7. Caesar had himself appointed _____ for life.

Down

1. Caesar was well liked by these people.
2. Cesar fell in love with _____.
3. Caesar led his army here; it is modern day France.
4. Caesar went to war with him and battled for 4 years.

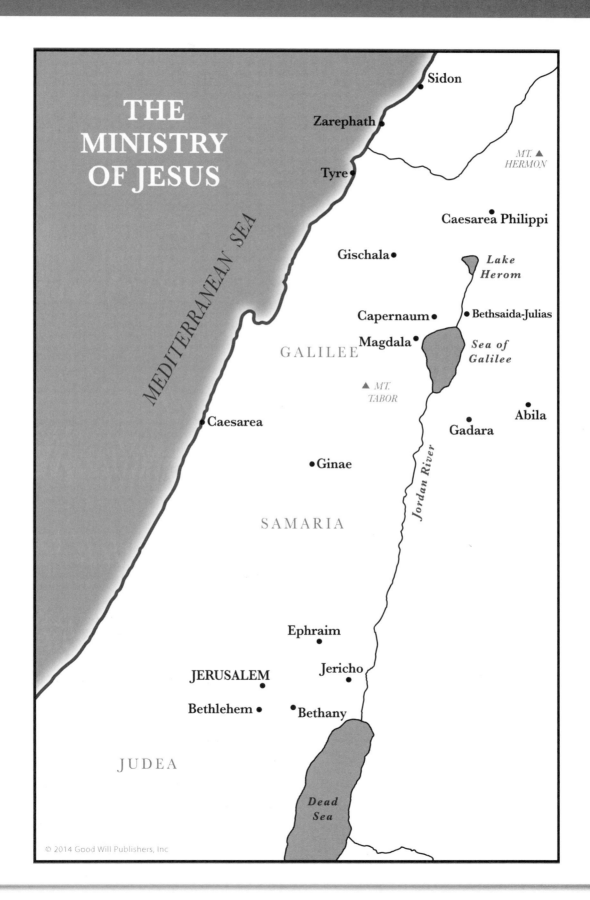

THE MINISTRY OF JESUS

MEDITERRANEAN SEA

Sidon

Zarephath

Tyre

MT. ▲ HERMON

Caesarea Philippi

Gischala

Lake Herom

GALILEE

Capernaum

Magdala

Bethsaida-Julias

Sea of Galilee

▲ *MT. TABOR*

Abila

Caesarea

Gadara

Jordan River

Ginae

SAMARIA

Ephraim

Jericho

JERUSALEM

Bethlehem

Bethany

JUDEA

Dead Sea

Across

3. Jesus says to give to ___ what belongs to Him.
7. The body and blood of Jesus.
12. A Roman province where Jesus began preaching.
13. Jesus calls himself the good _____.
14. This group especially disliked Jesus.

Down

1. Means messenger in Greek.
2. Jesus called _____ men to be disciples.
4. The crowds shouted this at Jesus.
5. Mother of Jesus.
6. State Mary was born in by a special grace of God.
8. Greek for Messiah.
9. Foster-father of Jesus.
10. King of Israel Joseph is descended from.
11. Jesus says to give to him what belongs to him.
15. Jesus grew up during his reigns.

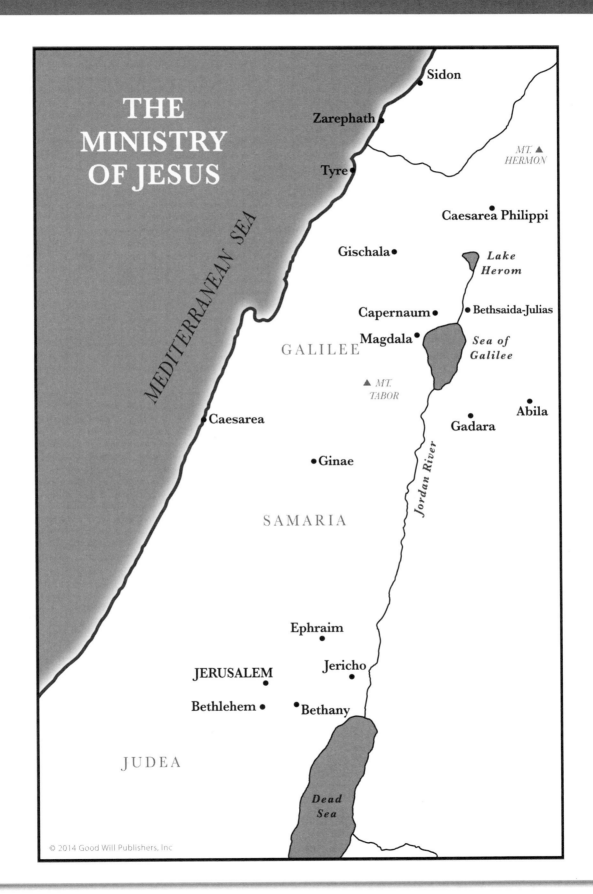

THE MINISTRY OF JESUS

MEDITERRANEAN SEA

Sidon

Zarephath

MT. ▲ HERMON

Tyre

Caesarea Philippi

Gischala

Lake Herom

Capernaum

Bethsaida-Julias

Magdala

Sea of Galilee

GALILEE

▲ MT. TABOR

Abila

Gadara

Caesarea

Jordan River

Ginae

SAMARIA

Ephraim

Jericho

JERUSALEM

Bethlehem

Bethany

JUDEA

Dead Sea

```
K M N R K E N B S R L I S F K S Y D
P X A C E E Z E I A Q E T I F N A A
G E O R V T L I N S V B N S G A D M
L R N A Y P E G T I H G F H R I D A
S A E T I M U P L P D O D E E T R S
L H S C E A A O T O A E P R A S I C
J E S R G C F G M N D B R S T I H U
C I G E E O O D N I C I O W R T S
D F S N T V F S E A M A E F I H B R
F V F N A G I C T J L Y S M N C M Y
M U U F O A S N V H H E T E D O O T
G O F D E A C H U R C H N N U W T R
M T I R I P S Y L O H N O C A E D A
R E S U R R E C T I O N P O P E Q M
J E R U S A L E M L U A P T N I A S
C I L O H T A C H U P A S S O V E R
H J F P F Y Y N L I S T I G P E Z S
C K J N Z E D J L X U A O M N T W J
```

Note: Some words may appear backwards. Find the following words. Recount the story of Jesus' life, death, and resurrection as you do: Angel, Ascended, Baptize, Bishop, Catholic, Christians, Church, Damascus, Deacon, Disciples, Fishers of Men, Great Wind, Heaven, Holy Spirit, Jerusalem, Kingdom of God, Languages, Martyrs, Mary Magdalen, Mount of Olives, Passover, Pentecost, Pope, Priest, Resurrection, Rock, Saint Paul, Saint Peter, Third Day, Tomb, Universal

TOEUCRRNIERS

JUSES SICTRH

NOS FO DOG

SEPNACRAEPA

LAL SINNATO

SOLTAPSE

NEIN SAYD

RIGNIV RAMY

SALT SPURPE

REAGT WIDN

LOYH TIPIRS

FDLIEL

PEKAS SNLUAGEGA

REHCAP

PATZEBDI

A	B	C	D	E	F	G	H	I	J	K	L	M	N	O	P	Q	R	S	T	U	V	W	X	Y	Z
		15				21									17			5				25			

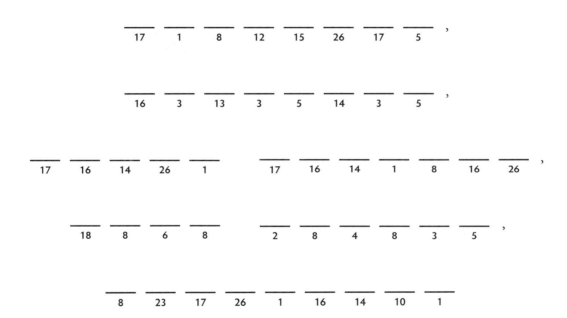

These were titles given to Octavian.

After cracking the code and filling in your answer, you should have a numeric symbol for most of the letters. Fill in a numeric symbol for the remaining letters of your own choosing and then write out a short coded message to your mom or dad below (you may want to use a scrap sheet of paper to practice your coded message). Give it to your parents for them to decipher.

Across
1. Tried to have his horse appointed consul.
4. Found hiding behind the curtains in the palace.
6. Made it a crime to speak baldly about the Emperor.
7. Killed Claudius in order to give Nero the throne.
8. Woman Augustus married.

Down
2. First Roman Emperor.
3. Family of Augustus and Livia.
5. Blamed the Christians for a great fire in Rome.

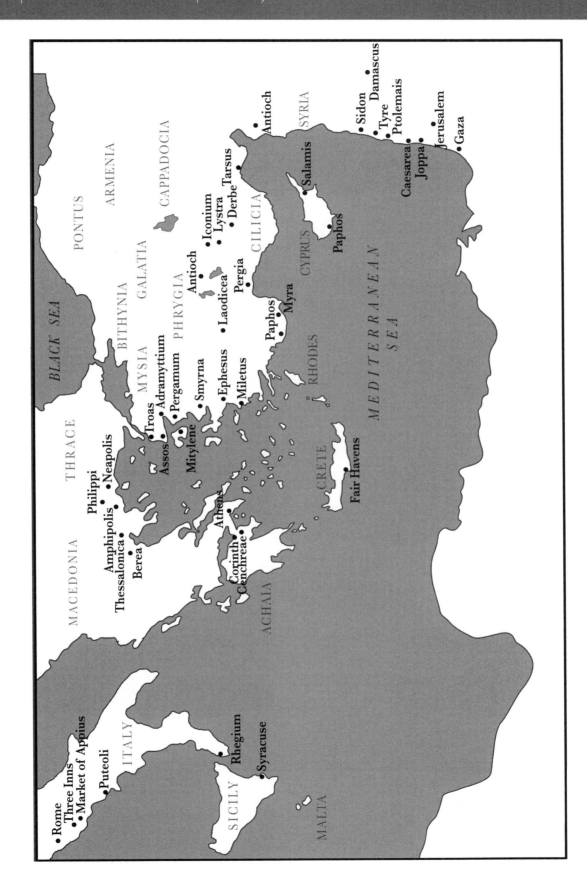

The Five "Good" Emperors Clues

1. _____ was a general and kind hearted man who was well liked.
2. Vespasian built the people of Rome a giant amphitheater called a _____.
3. In the Colosseum, you could watch _____ fights.
4. The Senate came together and selected one of their own to become emperor, a man named _____.
5. _____ conquered parts of Mesopotamia and what is now Romania.
6. _____ built a wall in northern England to separate Roman Britain from the barbarian north.
7. _____ _____ had such a peaceful reign that hardly anything was recorded while he was emperor.
8. _____ _____ spent his long reign fortifying the borders between 9._____ and 10. _____
11. None of these emperors were related to each other. Each one had _____ his successor.
12. The five men who ruled Rome are referred to as the "_____ _____."
13. They cared very much about _____ and 14. _____ and thus, there was 15. _____ for a long time.
16. A _____ is someone from outside the Roman Empire who did not have Roman culture.
17. These "good" emperors were not so "good" from a _____ point of view.
18. They had many Christians put to _____.
19. It was Trajan who had _____ _____ of Antioch put to death.
20. _____ fouled up everything his predecessors had worked to build.

The Five "Good" Emperors Word Search

```
S Y N A M R E G L V Q G S S J
D U H A D R I A N E H D U U U
N E I M I B A S W S V I I D S
C A A L B R U E C P T R P O T
O H J T E D A O W A D O S M I
A X R A H R L B N S P M U M C
A L J I R O U G R I M E N O E
Y D L C S T I A L A J G I C P
Y A O S F T Y W S N B A N H A
W X E P N V I F X U S U O L V
E U N I T P E A C E C P T G R
M C A A R E O S N N I R N M E
T S M N E I D E Q S L W A R N
G O O D E M P E R O R S T M E
R O T A I D A L G P D Z E U Z
```

Note: Some words may appear backwards. If you have trouble figuring out the words from your clues, see if you can find the words from this list: Adopted, Antoninus Pius, Barbarian, Christians, Colosseum, Commodus, Death, Germany, Gladiator, Good Emperors, Hadrian, Justice, Law, Marcus Aurelius, Nerva, Peace, Rome, Saint Ignatius, Trajan, Vespasian

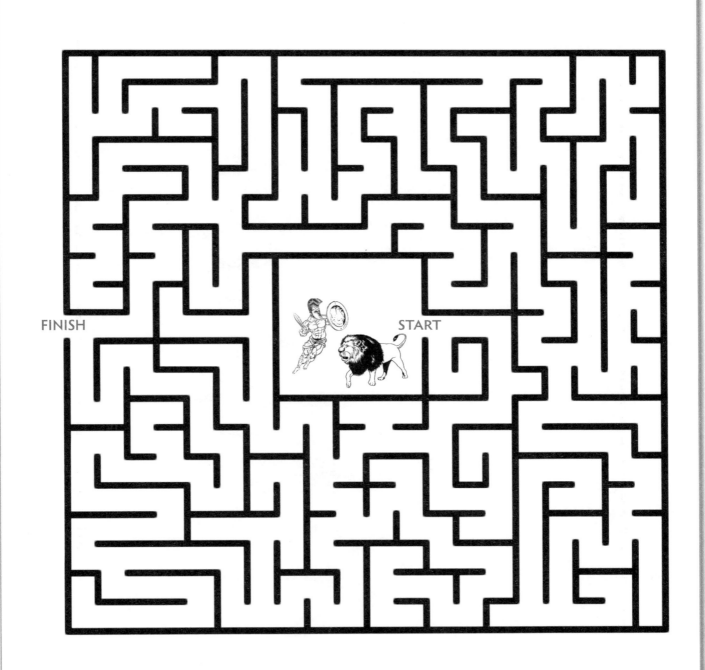

FINISH

START

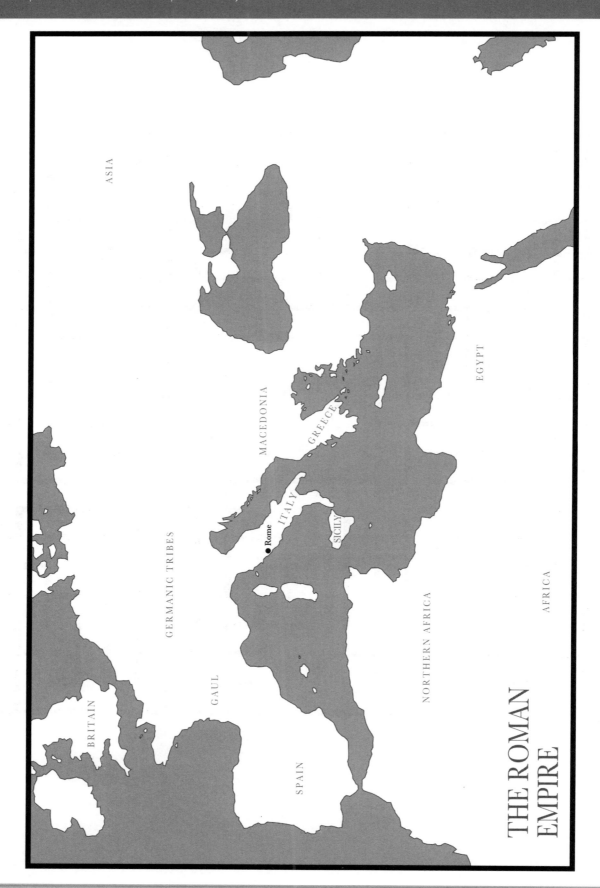

ASIA

EGYPT

MACEDONIA

GREECE

GERMANIC TRIBES

ITALY

●Rome

SICILY

NORTHERN AFRICA

AFRICA

BRITAIN

GAUL

SPAIN

THE ROMAN
EMPIRE

```
G  E  R  M  A  N  W  I  K  F  C  K  P
T  L  K  I  K  D  N  T  N  O  S  D  E
E  M  O  R  H  V  U  I  N  S  W  I  B
M  R  B  T  A  G  F  G  E  A  M  U  V
B  U  X  S  L  M  H  X  A  X  K  U  I
W  A  I  O  S  T  R  O  G  O  T  H  S
B  O  R  V  D  B  F  T  S  N  E  L  I
N  J  Y  B  R  Y  H  R  V  S  A  O  G
M  I  N  N  A  M  E  L  A  D  X  R  O
D  S  N  S  B  R  B  M  N  N  F  I  T
Z  Z  I  F  M  L  I  A  O  Q  K  J  H
P  A  I  C  O  B  V  A  Q  B  H  S  S
N  L  W  S  L  R  F  Y  N  R  Q  I  S
```

Note: Some words may appear backwards. Alemanni, Asian, Barbarian, Franks, German, Invasion, Lombards, Ostrogoths, Rome, Saxons, Vandals, Visigoths

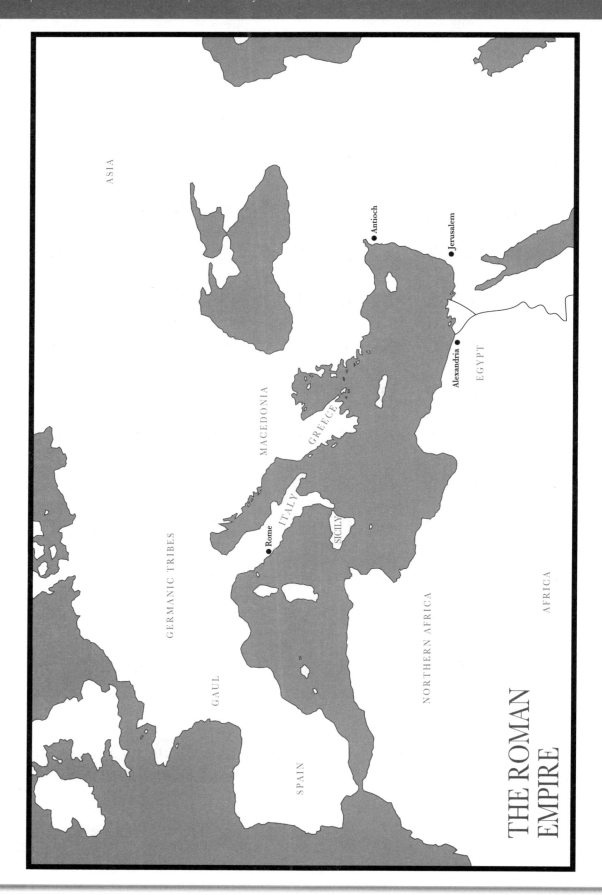

ASIA

Antioch

Jerusalem

Alexandria

EGYPT

MACEDONIA

GREECE

ITALY

SICILY

Rome

GERMANIC TRIBES

NORTHERN AFRICA

AFRICA

GAUL

SPAIN

THE ROMAN EMPIRE

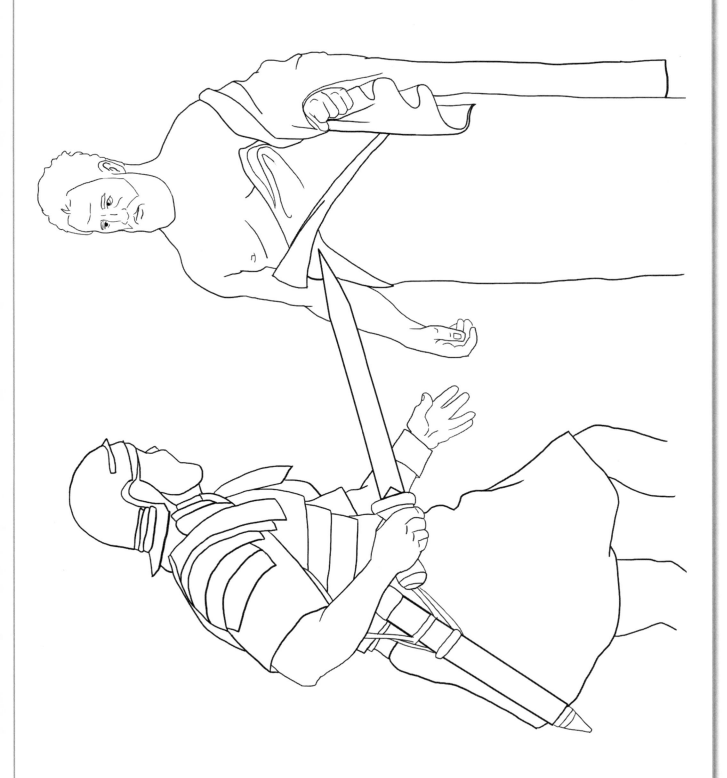

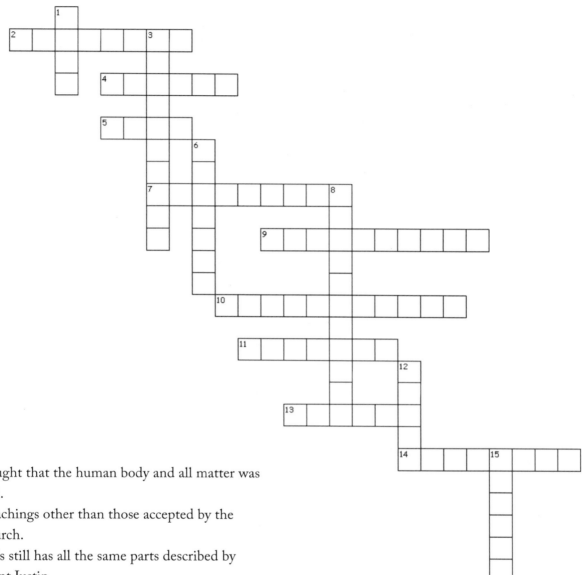

Across

2. Taught that the human body and all matter was evil.
4. Teachings other than those accepted by the church.
5. This still has all the same parts described by Saint Justin.
7. Writers who tried to explain Christianity to pagans.
9. Taught that the Father and Holy Spirit became man as well.
10. Believed that the God of the Old Testament and New Testament were different Gods.
11. The bishop of Carthage in North Africa.
13. Saint _____ offered one of the earliest written records of Christian worship.
14. This heresy taught that some sins couldn't be forgiven.

Down

1. The bishops of _____ were the successors of Peter.
3. The Romans viewed _____ as traitors.
6. In ancient Rome this meant an explanation.
8. Those who study and write about Christian theology.
12. Meeting of bishops where questions of theology and discipline are discussed.
15. The science or study of God and His revelation.

CITCOAHL HUCHCR

☐☐☐☐☐☐☐☐　☐☐☐☐☐☐
　　　1　　　5

STNAI SITJUN

☐☐☐☐☐☐　☐☐☐☐☐☐

SASM

☐☐☐☐

GIOPOSLAT

☐☐☐☐☐☐☐☐☐
　　　　4　7

SIAHNTIRC

☐☐☐☐☐☐☐☐☐
　2

TISNA NIARYPC

☐☐☐☐☐☐　☐☐☐☐☐☐☐
　　　　　　8

DYNSO

☐☐☐☐☐
　　6

SIOHPB

☐☐☐☐☐☐

SEYHER

☐☐☐☐☐☐
　　3

☐☐☐☐☐☐☐☐
1　2　3　4　5　6　7　8

A	B	C	D	E	F	G	H	I	J	K	L	M	N	O	P	Q	R	S	T	U	V	W	X	Y	Z
	7			6			9								18						1				

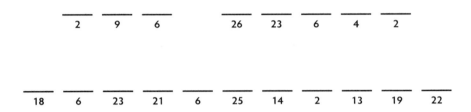

```
___  ___  ___        ___  ___  ___  ___  ___
 2    9    6          26   23   6    4    2


___  ___  ___  ___  ___  ___  ___  ___  ___  ___  ___
18    6   23   21    6   25   14    2   13   19   22
```

This ordered that all Christian churches be destroyed, and all copies of the Bible be handed over and burned. Christians were forbidden from gathering for worship. All bishops and clergy were to be imprisoned and all persons throughout the empire had to sacrifice to the gods or face arrest.

After cracking the code and filling in your answer, you should have a numeric symbol for most of the letters. Fill in a numeric symbol for the remaining letters of your own choosing and then write out a short coded message to your mom or dad below (you may want to use a scrap sheet of paper to practice your coded message). Give it to your parents for them to decipher.

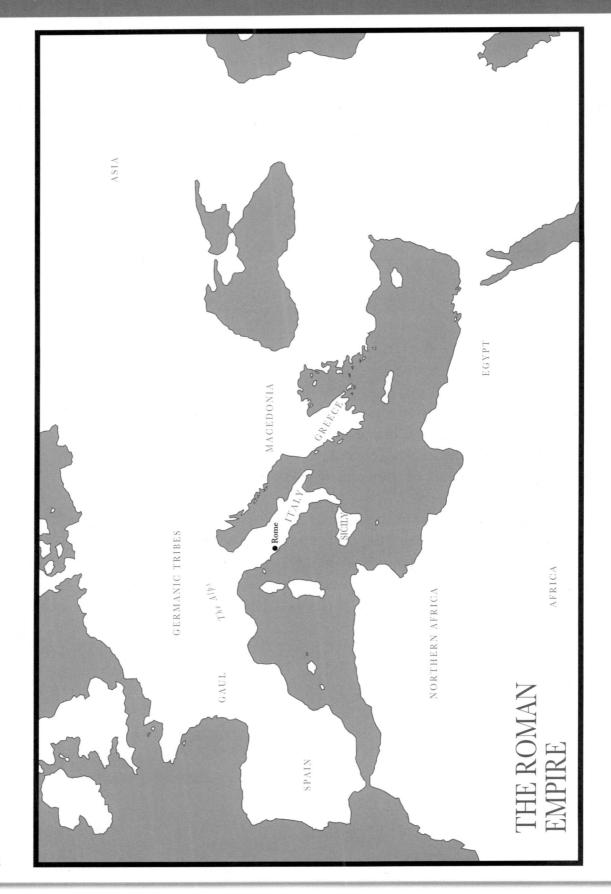

ASIA

EGYPT

MACEDONIA

GREECE

GERMANIC TRIBES

ITALY

•Rome

SICILY

The Alps

NORTHERN AFRICA

AFRICA

GAUL

SPAIN

THE ROMAN
EMPIRE

A	B	C	D	E	F	G	H	I	J	K	L	M	N	O	P	Q	R	S	T	U	V	W	X	Y	Z
8						24		2					26											10	

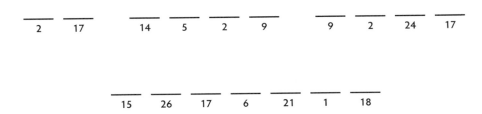

$$\overline{}\ \overline{}\quad \overline{}\ \overline{}\ \overline{}\ \overline{}\quad \overline{}\ \overline{}\ \overline{}\ \overline{}$$
2   17   14   5   2   9   9   2   24   17

$$\overline{}\ \overline{}\ \overline{}\ \overline{}\ \overline{}\ \overline{}\ \overline{}$$
15   26   17   6   21   1   18

Constantine ordered his solders to paint the chi-rho on their shields because he saw these words appear across the symbol.

After cracking the code and filling in your answer, you should have a numeric symbol for most of the letters. Fill in a numeric symbol for the remaining letters of your own choosing and then write out a short coded message to your mom or dad below (you may want to use a scrap sheet of paper to practice your coded message). Give it to your parents for them to decipher.

More from the *Story of Civilization* Series

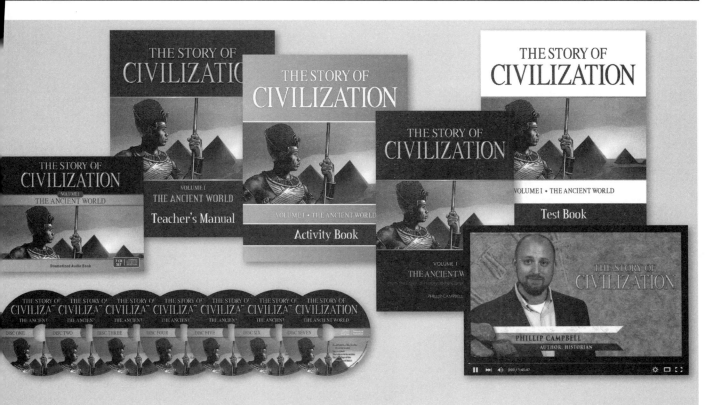

The Story of Civilization reflects a new emphasis in presenting the history of the world as a thrilling and compelling narrative. Within each chapter, children will encounter short stories that place them directly in the shoes of historical figures, both famous and ordinary, as they live through legendary battles and invasions, philosophical debates, the construction of architectural wonders, the discovery of new inventions and sciences, and the exploration of the world. *Volume I, The Ancient World,* begins the journey, covering the time periods from the dawn of history and the early nomads, to the conversion of Emperor Constantine. Children will learn what life was like in the ancient civilizations of Egypt, Mesopotamia, Persia, Greece, Rome, and more, as well as learn the Old Testament stories of the Israelites and the coming of Christ.

VOLUME I, THE ANCIENT WORLD

- TEXT BOOK: **$24.95**

- TEST BOOK: **$14.95**

- ACTIVITY BOOK: **$14.95**

- TEACHER'S MANUAL: **$19.95**

- ILLUSTRATED TIMELINE: **$14.95**

- AUDIO DRAMA: **$39.95**

- STREAMING VIDEO LECTURE SERIES: **$39.95**

- COMPLETE SET: **ONLY $154.70!**

TANBooks.com • (800) 437-5876

Children should not just read the Bible . . .

Volume I, The Old Testament, begins the journey. In these pages, children will visit the Garden of Eden, board Noah's ark, climb the Tower of Babel, follow Moses through the Red Sea, listen to David's harp, witness Samson's strength, enter the lion's den with Daniel, and learn God's plan from the prophets. Each account is told in storybook form to engage readers, with each narrative supplemented with actual Bible quotes. Your child's encounter with Scripture will never be the same!

VOLUME I, THE OLD TESTAMENT:

- TEXT BOOK: **$24.95**

- TEST BOOK: **$14.95**

- ACTIVITY BOOK: **$14.95**

- TEACHER'S MANUAL: **$19.95**

- AUDIO DRAMA: **$39.95**

- DVD LECTURES: **$39.95**

- COMPLETE SET: **ONLY $155.00!**